W9-BMG-898

The Teaching for Social Justice Series

William Ayers—Series Editor
Therese Quinn—Associate Series Editor

Editorial Board: Hal Adams, Barbara Bowman, Lisa Delpit,
Michelle Fine, Maxine Greene, Caroline Heller, Annette Henry,
Asa Hilliard, Rashid Khalidi, Gloria Ladson-Billings, Charles Payne,
Mark Perry, Luis Rodriguez, Jonathan Silin, William Watkins

Social Studies for Social Justice:
Teaching Strategies for the
Elementary Classroom
RAHIMA C. WADE

Pledging Allegiance:
The Politics of Patriotism
in America's Schools
JOEL WESTHEIMER, EDITOR

See You When We Get There:
Teaching for Change in Urban Schools
GREGORY MICHIE

Echoes of Brown:
Youth Documenting and Performing the
Legacy of Brown v. Board of Education
MICHELLE FINE

Writing in the Asylum:
Student Poets in City Schools
JENNIFER MCCORMICK

Teaching the Personal and the Political:
Essays on Hope and Justice
WILLIAM AYERS

Teaching Science for Social Justice
ANGELA CALABRESE BARTON, WITH
JASON L. ERMER, TANAHIA A. BURKETT,
AND MARGERY D. OSBORNE

Putting the Children First: The Changing
Face of Newark's Public Schools
JONATHAN G. SILIN AND
CAROL LIPPMAN, EDITORS

Refusing Racism: White Allies
and the Struggle for Civil Rights
CYNTHIA STOKES BROWN

A School of Our Own:
Parents, Power, and Community at the
East Harlem Block Schools
TOM RODERICK

The White Architects of Black Education:
Ideology and Power in America,
1865–1954
WILLIAM WATKINS

The Public Assault on America's
Children: Poverty, Violence,
and Juvenile Injustice
VALERIE POLAKOW, EDITOR

Construction Sites: Excavating Race,
Class, and Gender Among Urban Youths
LOIS WEIS AND
MICHELLE FINE, EDITORS

Walking the Color Line: The Art and
Practice of Anti-Racist Teaching
MARK PERRY

A Simple Justice:
The Challenge of Small Schools
WILLIAM AYERS, MICHAEL KLONSKY, AND
GABRIELLE H. LYON, EDITORS

Holler If You Hear Me: The Education of
a Teacher and His Students
GREGORY MICHIE

Social Studies for Social Justice

Teaching Strategies for the Elementary Classroom

RAHIMA C. WADE

FOREWORD BY

SONIA NIETO

LIBRARY
FRANKLIN PIERCE UNIVERSITY
RINDGE, NH 03461

TEACHERS
COLLEGE
PRESS

Teachers College
Columbia University
New York and London

Published by Teachers College Press, 1234 Amsterdam Avenue, New York, NY 10027

Copyright © 2007 by Teachers College, Columbia University

All rights reserved. No part of this publication may be reproduced or transmitted in any form or by any means, electronic or mechanical, including photocopy, or any information storage and retrieval system, without permission from the publisher.

Library of Congress Cataloging-in-Publication Data

Wade, Rahima C.
  Social studies for social justice : teaching strategies for the elementary classroom / Rahima C. Wade ; foreword by Sonia Nieto.
     p. cm. — (The teaching for social justice series)
  Includes bibliographical references and index.
  ISBN 978-0-8077-4762-9 (pbk. : alk. paper)
  1. Social sciences—Study and teaching (Elementary)—United States.   2. Social justice—Study and teaching (Elementary)—United States.   I. Title.
  LB1530.W288 2007
  372.83—dc22

                                                                            2006100455

ISBN 978-0-8077-4762-9 (paper)

Printed on acid-free paper

Manufactured in the United States of America

14   13   12   11   10   09   08   07   8   7   6   5   4   3   2   1

Contents

Series Foreword

In 1963, a young civil rights worker proposed to create a network of Freedom Schools across the South as a way to energize and focus the Civil Rights Movement. He noted that while Black students had been denied many things—decent facilities, fully trained teachers, forward-looking curricula—the fundamental injury was that they were denied the right to "think for themselves" about the conditions of their lives, how they came to be the way they were, and how things might be changed. This worker initiated a curriculum of questions: Why are we, students and teachers, in the freedom movement? What do we want that we don't have? What do we have that we want to keep? Pursuing these questions to their furthest limits taught the 3 R's and so much more: How to take oneself seriously as a thinking person; how to locate one's life in the contexts of history, politics, and economic conditions; how to imagine and then work toward a new society.

Over the next several years Freedom Schools were launched all over the country, and not just in schools, but also in community centers, churches, parks, coffee shops—in fact, anywhere people came together freely to face one another in dialogue. People got a taste of popular education, saw the dimensions of what a school for democracy and freedom might be, and teaching for social justice came fully to life. It was wild, unruly, and diverse, and yet its common edges were there for all to see: Teachers consciously became students of their students; students were active participants in their own learning—authors, artists, activists—rather than passive receptacles of someone else's ideas; teaching and learning was cast as having a larger purpose, and that purpose was the fullest participation possible in the world we share, including the development of capacities to change that world. Classrooms were characterized by their propulsive midwifery properties.

Teaching for social justice begins with the idea that every human being is entitled to decent standards of freedom and justice, and that any violation must be acknowledged, testified to, and opposed. Every human being is a gooey biological wonder, an unruly spark of meaning-making energy, the equal of every other human being. We try to hold in mind, then, a sense of the infinite and the ineffable tied up inexorably with the concrete and the real. We try to keep our eyes open to the largest images of humanity that we can conjure, and to a powerful sense of history as something being made and remade by actual people, including ourselves.

The challenge of teaching for social justice is this: to find the capacity to oppose injustice and stand up on behalf of the disadvantaged at a time when power is so consolidated and unfairly weighed against them. Our guides and ideals must be knowledge, enlightenment, and truth on the one hand, and on the other human freedom, emancipation, liberation for all, with an emphasis on the dispossessed. This is the core of humanism, unachievable in some ultimate or final form, but a standard within our existential boundaries, a focus for our best energy and effort.

We live in a time when the assault to disadvantaged communities is particularly harsh and at the same time gallingly obfuscated. Access to adequate resources and decent facilities, to relevant curricula, to opportunities to reflect on and to think critically about the world is unevenly distributed along predictable lines of class and color. Furthermore, a movement to dismantle public schools under the rubric of "zero tolerance," "standards and accountability," and "privatization" is in place and gaining force. This is the moment within which we have to choose who to be as teachers and as citizens.

Humanity is driven forward by a long, continuous "I don't know." It is, after all, not the known that pushes and pulls us along, although we must be serious about preparation, work, discipline, and labor. Teaching is hard work, and teachers often feel as if they crashed into a wall—an overwhelmed, uncertain, and deeply confused and dislocated intern. But if we stay with it, if we dive into the wreckage, we can find moments of relief, exhilaration, self-discovery, and even joy.

If we are to develop critical consciousness, we begin by knowing ourselves, in the words of Antonio Gramsci (1971), "as a product of the historic process to date, which has deposited in us an infinity of traces, without leaving an inventory" (p. 73). We must, furthermore, open our eyes to the world as it is—the enduring state of racism and the evermore elusive and intractable barriers to racial justice, the ongoing oppression of women wrapped up as often as not in the language of freedom, the targeting of gay and lesbian people as deviants and scapegoats, the rapidly widening gulf between rich and poor, and the enthronement of greed; we are faced as well with aggressive economic and military adventures abroad, and the violence of conquest and occupation from the Middle East and Central Asia to South America.

Teaching for social justice is more possibility than accomplishment, but it always involves themes of democracy, activism, self-awareness, imagination, opening public space, and participating in history. Social justice is surely about a fairer, more just distribution of social wealth and power, but it also aims at recognition, and at disruption of social structures that devalue and disrespect. Teachers working for social justice insist that all can grow to understand the world, and that each of us can connect our conduct to our consciousness.

There is a long tradition of teaching whose purpose is to combat silence, to defeat erasure and invisibility, to resist harm and redress grievances, to promote a more balanced, fair, and equitable order. Several questions can act as guideposts for this kind of teaching:

- What are the issues that marginalized or disadvantaged people speak of with excitement, anger, fear, or hope?
- How can I enter a dialogue in which I will learn from students about the problems and obstacles they face?
- What experience do students already have that can point the way toward solutions?
- What narrative is missing from the "official story" that will make the problems my students encounter more understandable?
- What current or proposed policies serve the privileged or the powerful, and how are they made to appear normal and inevitable?
- How can public space—in my classroom, in the larger community—for discussion, problem-posing and problem-solving, and fuller and wider participation be expanded?

Of course, there are others.

These kinds of questions are not a map, but they do point in a direction: We are, each of us, living in history, and we are, each of us, subjects *in*, not objects *of*, history; what we do or don't do makes a difference; each of us is a work-in-progress, trudging forward, in-process, unfinished. And in a world as out of balance as this one, each of us has work to do.

William C. Ayers
University of Illinois at Chicago

Therese Quinn
Art Institute of Chicago

REFERENCE

Gramsci, A. (1971). *Selections from the prison notebooks of Antonio Gramsci* (Q. Hoare & G. Nowell Smith, Eds. and Trans.). New York: International Publishers.

Foreword

Teachers do have a lot on their plate these days: With preparing students to take high-stakes tests, learning the state standards and applying them to the curriculum, and keeping abreast of all the local, state, and national mandates—not to mention actually teaching, collecting lunch money, planning field trips, and communicating with families, among many other tasks—where on earth are they supposed to find the time to even *think* about including a social justice perspective in their teaching? The premise of *Social Studies for Social Justice* is that teachers *must* find the time to do so because good teaching goes beyond bureaucratic responsibilities and directives. In fact, as Rahima Wade makes clear in this book, education should be first and foremost about teaching core values of respect and responsibility, commitment to service to others, and care for and about human life and the environment. Because a social justice education teaches youngsters to value and model dignity and decency, using social justice as a framework for the curriculum will in the long run make a greater difference in the lives of children, teachers, and the nation than will passing a test or mastering the latest science experiment.

Although the focus here is on social studies, social justice teaching is about both content and an approach, one that can inform all subject matters. Beginning with kindergarten and lasting throughout the grades, it includes everything from lessons and units to room arrangements and the selection of children's literature, and it encompasses all levels of activity from reading about social change to participating in creating it. Rahima Wade, however, is not interested in simply presenting readers with abstract principles. What is most satisfying about this book are the many powerful examples of social justice teaching in classrooms by elementary-school teachers around the country. From Melinda's "kids who care" classroom to Rob's fifth graders who investigate which U.S. presidents were slave owners, social justice teaching is exciting, revealing, and engaging. It is, in the end, about creating a classroom environment of respect, care, and responsibility.

Teaching with a social justice perspective, as Rahima Wade reminds us, is not always easy. As will become clear from the numerous examples throughout the book, teachers must sometimes defy conventional wisdom and traditional practice to create social justice classrooms. Many times, they must "think outside the box" to design curriculum that fits the standards while also going beyond them. And they must sometimes challenge expectations about what it means to teach social studies in the elementary grades. While some may think of social justice teaching as both depressing and discouraging, this book challenges that perception by bringing to light many illustrations that are joyful and positive.

Rahima Wade is no stranger to social justice teaching. As an elementary-school teacher herself in New Hampshire a couple of decades ago, she created a learning environment in which all her students were valued and cared for. She later brought this same perspective to her work as a teacher educator, and now, happily for the readers of this book, she has brought it to a larger audience through the examples of teachers around the country who teach with a social justice lens. One of the greatest lessons of this powerful book is that teachers can make a life-defining difference in the lives of their students by teaching them to stand on the side of social justice. As the old adage goes, "If you don't stand for something, you'll fall for anything." *Social Studies for Social Justice* will help teachers learn how to stand with their students for creative and life-affirming social change.

Sonia Nieto

Preface

It is easy to become disheartened when considering the many problems that beset our world. Perhaps you are like me: You worry about the environment, bemoan the level of addiction among our youth, and feel overwhelmed by the numbers of people who are homeless and hungry, out of work, or dying of AIDS. You wish there was something you could do. But life is busy and demanding; all you can manage most days is to go to work and take care of your family or spend some time with your friends. Despite your concerns for the state of the world, you often avoid the news because it is so depressing. You rationalize that at least you are a teacher. You are doing your part to help young people become informed, productive, and active members of society.

It is true that teaching is a profession with the potential for making a difference. Most of us can point to teachers who have made a big impact on our lives, someone who has inspired us, who has been able to see our potential. Good teaching makes a difference in the lives of students in small and large ways, every day, in schools all over the world.

This book is about good teaching, but not just good for children. Teaching for social justice is also good for the planet. This work has two goals: to make a difference both for children and for the world they will soon inherit. Teaching for social justice asks us to care deeply for the children we teach, and in doing so, to remember that none of us is truly separate from another. Communities thrive when everyone has a job and a place to live, wholesome food and clean water, the opportunity to voice our concerns and the chance to work together to solve the problems at hand. None of us can live well without the support of others, and all of us are better off when our community as a whole is a safe, healthful, and productive place to live.

Teaching for social justice is not just about preparing children for high school and college and their careers beyond. It is also about preparing them to be stewards of their world, to develop the skills, knowledge, and values to make our world a worthwhile and livable place for everyone, regardless of one's ethnicity, gender, age, size, sexual orientation, religion, social class, or physical ability.

If your heart sings when you consider that you can be a teacher *and* make a contribution to creating a just and healed world, this book is for you. Opening to the possibility that teaching elementary social studies could contribute to solving world hunger or finding a cure for AIDS may seem like a stretch, but dedicated teachers everywhere are teaching children every day with such goals in mind.

Dedication to social justice teaching is an important first step, yet putting one's ideals into practice in American schools and communities is a challenging task. This book goes beyond theory and idealistic views about the nature of social justice teaching to embrace the full spectrum of teachers' social justice teaching experiences. Informed by the experiences of more than 40 elementary school teachers across the country, this book is designed to serve as a practical resource for elementary school teachers and preservice teachers in elementary teacher education programs who aim to teach for and about social justice.

Chapter 1 makes the case for social justice teaching in the elementary social studies curriculum. Chapter 2 explores the nature of social justice and the essential characteristics of social justice education. The information in both of these chapters sets the context for the ideas and teaching practices discussed in the rest of the book.

In Chapter 3 I focus on strategies for creating socially just classroom communities. Social justice education is concerned with respectful relating and building a supportive and collaborative class community. Creating a just classroom involves providing frequent opportunities for student voice and choice, as well as using strategies for group decision making and problem solving.

Chapter 4 explains how to approach the teaching of social studies and deal with the challenges of district-mandated curricula and statewide standards and tests. Sources of support include colleagues, parents, and the school culture. Teaching for social justice is not always easy; yet there are many creative options for meeting the ever-present challenges. Social justice in action is featured in two stories of teachers' classroom practice.

In Chapter 5 I address the content of the social studies curriculum and the topics and skills important in social justice education. These topics fall into three broad categories: human rights, democracy, and conservation. Among the skills discussed are how to "read the world" and how to effectively engage in activism. A unit on the Civil Rights Movement illustrates how to effectively combine both content and skills to accomplish social justice goals.

Chapter 6 focuses on essential in-class strategies for teaching social justice. A wide variety of teaching strategies are discussed, including children's literature, questions, role-plays and simulations, primary sources, and the arts.

In Chapter 7 I explore strategies for connecting students with social justice in the real world beyond the classroom. It is important to provide students with firsthand opportunities to learn about and work for social justice on the local level, from addressing injustices in the school to welcoming guest speakers, to involving students out in the community via rallies, marches, and service-learning projects.

Chapter 8 focuses on the many paths taken to social justice teaching and the continuing opportunities for learning and growth available to us as educators. From travel to collegial associations, to independent inquiry, occasions for nurturing and supporting social justice ideals can be found in communities everywhere.

Appendix A is a list of children's literature books, curriculum materials, and Web sites for social justice education in elementary social studies. Many of the teachers in the study contributed resource suggestions for this list. Finally, Appendix B provides details on the research study that informed the ideas in the book. The description includes teacher demographics, copies of the research invitation and questions, and a discussion of the methods for collecting and analyzing teacher interviews.

Acknowledgments

Many people helped shape this book, but it would not have been written without the daily efforts of teachers all over the country who teach for and about social justice. I especially want to thank the 40 teachers who contributed their time in sharing with me about their social justice teaching. I was privileged to learn from them, and I was continually inspired by their dedication and creativity; they are my heroes and heroines.

I am also grateful to the National Council for the Social Studies for a CUFA-FASSE inquiry grant award that allowed me to engage in more in-depth work with 10 of the 40 teachers. Our weekend together allowed us to dive deeper into the heart of social justice teaching, to explore the essentials of this work, and to make meaningful and lasting connections with each other.

A number of people at Teachers College Press lent their expertise to making this book more practical and accessible. I want to thank especially Carole Saltz, Bill Ayers, Therese Quinn, Judy Berman, and the anonymous reviewers for their advice and feedback throughout the process of shaping the ideas and format of the book.

And finally, to you, the readers, I extend my thanks for your interest in teaching for social justice. My sincere hope is that you will find the ideas in this book useful in guiding your students both to live productive and healthy lives and to help create a better world for us all.

1

Introduction

In less than the time it will take you to read this page, two children will die of malaria, one mother will die during pregnancy, and three people will die of tuberculosis. And those are just the statistics from Africa. Looking at the numbers on a global scale is mind-numbing: Nine million people will die this year due to hunger and malnutrition, 5 million of them children. In fact, more than a billion people suffer from hunger across the globe. Each day more than 8,000 people are infected by HIV/AIDS. And those are just the world health statistics. If we look at the data on the environment, crime, war, literacy rates, and so on, we face an equally grim reality of escalating problems worldwide.

But what do these issues have to do with teaching elementary-school children? Don't elementary-school teachers have more than enough to handle in teaching, counseling, and managing children in their classrooms each day? And how are young children to understand or influence global problems whose solutions often mystify adult citizens, the private sector and government officials alike?

While at first it might seem that social justice education should be relegated to graduate schools and expert think tanks, it is precisely because these problems are so overwhelming and seemingly intractable that we must start at the earliest levels of schooling. If students are to develop a commitment to social justice ideals, this work should begin in the elementary years when children are concerned with fairness and when their empathy and perspective-taking abilities are in the formative stages.

Starting in kindergarten, we must educate youth to care about humanity and to begin to comprehend the immensity of the challenges that will face them as adults. We must embark upon teaching them the skills and knowledge that will ultimately enable them not only to live productive and empowered lives themselves, but also to work alongside like-minded others for the betterment of those who suffer from oppression and other inequities. In other words, we must teach both about and for social justice, for the children in our classrooms and for the world to which we all belong.

You may ask, "Couldn't we wait until at least high school? Don't children deserve to be protected from such problems in their early years?" If only this were possible! While the statistics cited above are more representative of life in developing countries, many children in the United States are no strangers to poverty, hunger, or racism. Hundreds of thousands of children across the country live the experience of oppression and injustice on a daily basis. And ignoring this fact will do nothing to change it. As teachers, we have an obligation to help our students develop the skills, knowledge, and values to create a society that will someday no longer tolerate the abject poverty of so many amidst the luxury of the few.

The more pertinent dilemma in regard to social justice education in the elementary classroom is not *whether* to teach for social justice but rather *how* to do so effectively. What does it look like in practice? Does elementary social justice teaching find kindergartners studying the African AIDS epidemic or third graders learning about the atrocities of the Iraq war? These are not easy questions. Of course, the decision about how much of humanity's distress to expose to one's students depends on many factors. Every social justice lesson takes place within a context: a classroom, a school, a community, and a curriculum—all with a set of values, limitations, or requirements that influence both the choices we make and the outcomes of our efforts.

Yet successful teaching for social justice never involves ignoring children's developmental needs or neglecting their psychological and emotional well-being. Appropriate social justice lessons will consider children's abilities and interests as well as a teacher's desire to stretch the boundaries of students' caring and understanding.

Besides, effective social justice teaching is so much more than lessons about AIDS in Africa. It's about relating respectfully, allowing student voice and choice, building a cohesive classroom community, and facilitating collaboration and conflict resolution. It's about encouraging empathy, thinking outside of the box, coming up with creative solutions, and taking action in the school and community. Teaching for social justice embraces paradox. It's about honoring both individual needs and the common good, advocating for long-term social change while also alleviating a bit of the suffering in our midst. And it's about learning the skills to be successful in contemporary society while also garnering the tools to change that same society for the better.

Whether you are a beginning teacher or a seasoned veteran, teaching in an urban, suburban, or rural school, in a wealthy district or an impoverished community, you can effectively teach for and about social justice with students of all ages. Social justice teaching can be practical, creative, and developmentally appropriate. With passion and creativity, we can bring to life the three Rs, meet state standards, and encourage our students' academic success, while also planting the seeds for social change.

In the time it will take you to read this page, hundreds—perhaps thousands—of elementary-school teachers are taking their next steps toward bringing about an equitable and just world. While holding a class meeting or teaching a lesson on prejudice may at first glance seem to be a far cry from solving the problem of global poverty, this work is one of small yet significant steps. Elementary children are developing empathy, learning from multiple perspectives, and working on issues of importance to them in their schools and communities. And students in social justice classrooms will hopefully become adults who have the vision, commitment, and skills to create solutions to difficult problems, and the perseverance to make those ideas a reality.

Significant global change will require the commitment of millions of citizens around the world. Many more social justice teachers are necessary if we are to create a just and equitable society. With no exclusive requirements, there is room for all to take part. With every act, every teacher, every lesson, and every student, social justice teaching provides greater promise and possibility for the future. Consider yourself invited; make a commitment to the challenging and important endeavor of creating empowered students and a socially just world.

2

Understanding Social Justice Education

The term *social justice* is often used, but rarely defined. Ask a group of educators what words come to mind in regard to the concept of social justice and you are likely to hear descriptors of *injustice*—words such as *oppression, poverty, discrimination*, and *racism*. It is much easier for us to wrap our minds around what an all-too-familiar unjust society looks like than to conjure up a clear image of the illusive and distant goal of a socially just world.

Yet if we are to teach for and about social justice, understanding what it looks, sounds, and feels like is critical. A lucid picture of this concept is essential to guide our curricular decisions, our relationships with students, and our building of a socially just classroom community. We must therefore explore the complexity of social justice in order to arrive at a working definition of the term that will serve as a necessary backdrop to a discussion of the essential elements of social justice education.

THE NATURE OF SOCIAL JUSTICE

The task of defining social justice in a way that makes it concrete, meaningful, and useful in the elementary classroom is a formidable challenge. Contemporary educators approach understanding social justice from vastly different perspectives, including Marxist, feminist, postmodern, humanist, critical, and ecological. One can easily get lost in the swirl of these ideas, many of which seem more suited to the realms of politics and law than teaching. Unfortunately, the literature on the nature of social justice does little to help us settle on a suitable definition for the elementary classroom.

Writers on social justice have always debated its meaning. Scholars and theologians in the early 1900s wrote of social justice as either *distributive justice*—the promotion of the common good or distribution of goods according to equity—*legal justice*—citizens' allegiance to each other's rights and society as a whole—or some combination of the two (Willoughby, 1900). Others have contended that social justice requires a charitable perspective beyond that necessitated by law (Pipkin, 1927). A more recent argument asserts that social justice should be about how we relate to and treat each other, both in face-to-face interactions and in macro social and economic relations (Young, 1990).

Is social justice about equity, equality, happiness, caring, difference, or power? What is more important, the "common good" or living the good life? Is social justice possible within a capitalist society? What are the roles of the individual and the institution in bringing about social change? Can we fully understand social justice separate from ecological justice? Is social justice a verb or a noun? Is it more about personal empowerment or planetary healing? These questions are just a few of the many that emerge from the diversity of ideas and positions in the literature.

The definition of social justice I am about to offer does not fit neatly into any one perspective, nor does it address all of the questions and concerns that arise in the literature. It does, however, provide a practical focus for elementary classroom teachers to work for in their classrooms and community. It is born of my own and other teachers' experiences in attempting to concretize this elusive term. I define *social justice* as the process of working toward, and the condition of, meeting everyone's basic needs and fulfilling everyone's potential to live productive and empowered lives as participating citizens of our global community. "Basic needs" include not just food, clothing, and shelter, but also feeling safe, secure, and cared for. Fulfilling our potential requires education and health care, as well as respect, dignity, and the opportunity to pursue our dreams.

The position set forth in this book is that social justice is both personal *and* planetary, both practical *and* visionary, and both process *and* goal. Social justice is concerned with equitable distribution of resources as well as relating to each other with respect and care. Teaching for and about social justice calls upon us to embrace these seeming dualities as we teach individual children in our classrooms day to day and, at the same time, work toward the vision of a socially just world. Social justice is incompatible with oppression or discrimination based on race or ethnicity, social class, gender, sexual orientation, religion, age, or intellectual or physical ability. At the core of social justice lies both the belief in the equal worth of every person as well as the willingness to act from a place of both morality and care in upholding that belief. In a socially just society, every person is treated according to his or her need toward the goal of becoming a capable and contributing member of that society.

The roots of injustice can be found both in individual actions and in societal institutions where privilege creates unequal treatment of people. While changing beliefs and individual actions are effective strategies in working for social justice, significant progress can be made only when many of us work together within larger social and political movements.

But which is more important, to foster social justice among the children in our classrooms or to work for social justice in the world? Fortunately, these goals are one and the same. Informed by a vision of a socially just society, we work to create a socially just classroom community. And teaching children the skills, knowledge, and values needed to work for a socially just world, they grow to be cocreators of that dream. Social justice is about the day-to-day ways that we relate to our students, how we give them a voice in their learning, and our efforts to treat them according to their needs and abilities. At the same time, we must work for social justice in the world. Social justice is an ideal, a vision, a goal we have not just for our students, but for everyone, and especially for those who live with the reality or threat of hunger, poverty, illness, and oppression on their doorstep.

In fact, if we privilege either fostering social justice in the classroom or fostering social justice in the world to the exclusion of the other, we limit the power and promise of social justice education. If we focus only on creating a socially just classroom, we may neglect teaching students the skills and strategies for creating a socially just world. On the other hand, if we direct our attention solely to developing a socially just society beyond the classroom, we are at risk for indoctrinating our students toward certain political perspectives and ignoring the essential elements of what students can learn about social justice through their daily interactions in the classroom community.

In the microcosm of the elementary classroom, we discover that we can actualize many of the ideals of a socially just world—at least on our good days. Children can share resources fairly, listen respectfully, voice their opinions, make collective decisions, and develop the skills to live productive lives and to work for societal change. In the elementary classroom, social justice transforms from an abstract and distant possibility to a lived experience, albeit with the conflicts and problems that accompany any attempt to live and work with others who hold differing values, needs, and interests.

CARE AND FAIRNESS

Our students may be able to relate more clearly to the concept of social justice if we focus on two of its central features: *care* and *fairness*. Children understand these terms and their importance in their daily lives. Care and fairness are taught at home and at school, and children refer to them in play.

A focus on care can help students realize and act on their connections with others, both in the classroom and in the wider world. Inherent in social justice is a sense of relating to others with respect, dignity, and empathy. According to educators Burke-Hengen and Smith (2000), "Ethical thinking and behavior are grounded in a sense of interconnectedness. Because we have the capacity to grasp our relatedness to others, we seek to protect them from harm and preserve their happiness. . . . For us, the willingness to work for social justice is based on the capacity to care" (p. 100). In other words, caring for others leads naturally to working for others' rights and well-being.

The second key element, fairness, is something children develop a keen interest in at a young age. How often have we heard our students protest, "That's not fair"? However, most children tend to believe that fairness involves treating everyone the same. A more defensible position in regard to social justice harkens back to Marx's (1875/1972) idea, "from each according to his ability, to each according to his need." The elementary classroom provides an ideal setting for helping children realize that some people need more or different kinds of assistance if everyone is to have an equal opportunity to learn. Fairness must be informed by caring to arrive at the most suitable accommodations for each student.

CHARACTERISTICS OF SOCIAL JUSTICE EDUCATION

With care and fairness as core themes, let's look at some of the essential characteristics in the classroom practice of social justice teaching. There are two principal ways to approach social justice education. First, we can teach *about* social justice, exploring the legacy of injustice and justice in our nation's history and in the world. Second, we can teach *for* social justice, giving our students the skills, knowledge, and attitudes to live empowered lives themselves and to work for the basic human rights of all people. Practicing exemplary social justice education involves taking on both of these pursuits.

To be authentic and relevant for students, social justice education needs to begin with children's lived experiences—their concerns, hopes, and dreams—and then move toward multiple perspectives and action directed toward social change (Adams, Bell, & Griffin, 1997; Bigelow, Christensen, Karp, Miner, & Peterson, 1994). Beginning with children's experiences involves acknowledging and working from their cultural and linguistic resources, as well as their knowledge and interests (Cochran-Smith, 2004). The following characteristics of social justice education are essential to this work. Quality social justice education is student-centered, collaborative, experiential, intellectual, critical, multicultural, and activist (Bigelow et al., 1994; Wade, 2001, 2004). We will explore each of these in turn, considering both the rationale behind the characteristic and an example in practice, based on a third-grade unit on homelessness.

Social Justice Education Is Student-Centered

When we create a classroom community in which students feel valued and respected, they will be more likely to share their ideas and concerns openly and collaborate on issues of importance to them. We evidence our commitment to social justice when we practice integrity in relationships, generosity, and fairness and treat every student as a valued and whole person. Also, no matter what subject is being taught, the curriculum should focus on students' lives—their experiences, concerns, and needs—as well as on the particular subject matter (Christensen & Karp, 2003). Connecting the curriculum to students' prior knowledge is important for several reasons. In addition to the value, respect, and safety students experience in a student-centered classroom, research on constructivist teaching and learning tells us that learning is a process of human construction. "In this interpretive process, learners use their prior knowledge and beliefs—which they store in memory as mental structures . . . to make sense of the new input. . . . As this suggests, children's pre-existing knowledge, derived from personal and cultural experiences, is what gives them access to learning" (Villegas & Lucas, 2002, p. 73).

Thus a unit on homelessness in a third-grade classroom could begin with encouraging children to share what they know from their experience. Assuring children that there are no right or wrong answers, we can listen to their stories of encountering people who are homeless on the street. What happened? How did they feel? What did they do? We can also ask students to share their thoughts on why people are homeless and what types of assistance they need. These ideas can lead to generating questions to guide the development of future unit lessons.

Social Justice Education Is Collaborative

As teachers, we know that learning is enhanced through social interaction. Children can learn more if they are working alongside a teacher, an aide, or another, more capable peer. Vygotsky (1978) labeled this phenomenon "the zone of proximal development." Collaborative learning introduces children to new ideas and learning strategies they would not have encountered in independent work.

Beyond enhancing students' opportunities to learn, collaboration is important in social justice education for other reasons. For example, collaborative learning can contribute to interethnic understanding and solidarity (Nieto, 1999). Also, working with others reflects how people create change in the real world. Few of us work in isolation; even the greatest leaders in history were most effective in improving society when they worked in concert with strong coalitions of like-minded people. In the social justice classroom, students collaborate with each other and community partners to solve problems, mediate conflicts, and bring about social change.

In a third-grade unit on homelessness, students might work together in small groups of three or four to develop a plan for addressing one of the root causes of homelessness. Each small group could contact at least one community member, via phone or e-mail, who could share with them some expert advice about the issue under study, be it affordable housing, free health care, or raising the minimum wage.

Social Justice Education Is Experiential

Experiential learning requires a change from traditional forms of instruction in which students have little opportunity to take responsibility or initiative for their own education. Active participation in social justice education is essential for at least two reasons. First, learning is an active and constructive process through which we develop meaning based on our personal experience and our reflections on life. If young students only talk, read, or write about social justice, the depth of their understanding of social justice issues will be limited. They need to engage with social justice themes and issues experientially, through service projects as well as role-plays, mock trials, simulations, and the like. Through these modes of active learning, students experience key concepts and ideas in physically and emotionally engaging ways that bring social justice issues to life and allow them to learn, both intellectually and emotionally, in a deeper way.

Second, social justice can at times seem abstract and distant from students' lives. In order to make social justice "up close and personal," students need to be actively involved with others in the school and community, not only learning about injustice but also working together to create further social justice. As students work for social justice in their community, they should reflect on their experiences to maximize their learning and potential for positive social change in the future.

In the homelessness unit, students could participate in a simulation on losing one's home and trying to navigate the social welfare system to get food stamps, find a job, and rent an apartment. This simulation could be followed up with a guest speaker from the local homeless shelter, who would further enlighten the students about the challenges faced by people who are homeless in the community. Finally, students could reflect on both of these experiences through a class discussion and writing journal responses to the following questions: What are the difficulties faced by people who are homeless in getting their basic needs met? Which services are currently available and which are needed in our community?

Social Justice Education Is Intellectual

It is important to note that education for social justice should be academically rigorous. Teaching for social justice involves giving all students opportunities for significant intellectual work that requires them to think both critically and creatively. "A social justice classroom equips children not only to change the world but also to maneuver in the one that exists" (Bigelow et al., 1994, p. 5). Social justice education is seen as the means for students to learn and apply skills and knowledge in social studies, science, reading, writing, and math, toward the goal of creating a socially just society. Students are immersed in challenging cognitive work as they seek out a variety of perspectives on an issue and attempt to make sense of the different views and the implications they hold for possible social action projects. As students use their acquired skills and knowledge in attempting to solve real-world dilemmas, they are also actively engaged in challenging prevailing social and political norms and using creative imagination and critical thinking to devise new approaches to solving persistent public problems. These types of intellectual work contribute to academic achievement far beyond that typically measured by grades and standardized tests.

Students in a third-grade unit on homelessness could be engaged with a variety of data on the subject. Through completing math problems using unemployment and housing data and exploring facts and figures from several Web sites, they can learn about homelessness nationwide. Lessons in the unit could focus on learning about the many causes of homelessness and the complex issues involved in solving this pervasive problem in our society.

Social Justice Education Is Critical

Critique is a vital part of social justice education. Analyzing the roots of inequality in the curriculum, the school, and the society is a central step in working for social change. We must ask students to critique prevailing norms, to examine underlying assumptions and values, and to explore their own roles in relation to social problems. Students should have multiple opportunities to question social reality through critiques of advertising, cartoons, literature, legislation, foreign policy, job structures, and school life itself (Christensen & Karp, 2003). As they discover various sources of information, students consider whose voices are left out, who makes the decisions, and how to best effect change. High-quality social justice education requires youth "to develop their democratic capacities: to question, to challenge, to make real decisions, to collectively solve problems" (Bigelow et al., 1994, p. 4). If we wish to foster citizens who will actually improve, rather than just participate in, our democratic society, teaching students how to effectively critique their world is essential.

While critique and controversy often go hand in hand, we need not recoil from the challenges inherent in questioning authority. Instead, we can remember that every classroom decision involves values. As we recognize this fact, we can welcome differences of opinion among our students. It is important that we respect students' views when they differ from our own and at times challenge students to defend their views in light of how these views support (or do not support) social justice.

Levine (1995) reminds us that fostering critique requires both embracing controversy and being willing to take a stand:

> If we want to encourage the artful cultivation of democracy, we will acknowledge the value-laden nature of education and seek responsible ways to let conflict and discussion unfold in our classrooms. In part, this means helping students reflect critically on their own thoughts and feelings about big issues: racism, sexism, ecology, violence, distribution of wealth, the role of the United States around the world. But it also means sharing our own opinions on these issues with students, not as the final arbiters of truth, but as what we are in reality—thinking and feeling human beings with our own impulses and obligations to stand up for what we believe. (p. 57)

Third-grade students will undoubtedly have different views on the causes of homelessness, the degree of obligation we have to address this enormous problem, and the best ways to go about meeting the needs of homeless people in our community. Students can learn about current efforts from local policy makers and community agencies, and we could then engage students in questioning prevailing practices and searching for new ideas. At some point in the conversation, we can offer our own views, not in a heavy-handed attempt to convince students that our views are right, but to provide them with a model for both developing an informed opinion and taking a public stand.

Social Justice Education Is Multicultural

Social justice education is concerned with a conscious and consistent focus on including the history and perspectives of all people, including those with different ethnicities, physical abilities, religious beliefs, genders, sexual orientations, and socioeconomic situations. That history is often one of oppression and discrimination. "Multiculturalism is at the center of the struggle for fairness," noted Herbert Kohl (1994a,

p. 96). When we teach about multicultural issues authentically, we must of necessity focus on issues of power, oppression, and justice.

Cultural context and historical moment shape our understandings of events and how to respond; thus the various perspectives brought to the curriculum greatly influence students' views of an issue and the ideas they might have about how to effect positive social change. With the awareness that intolerant beliefs are among the root causes of injustice in society, teachers must work to ensure that all cultures have a place at the table. At the same time, different perspectives and cultural practices should be held up to the light of public standards, such as the "common good" or universal human rights. It is not enough to say that every cultural perspective makes a legitimate and acceptable contribution and leave it at that. We must move beyond "celebrating diversity" or "promoting tolerance" to helping our students understand how some differences lead to power, privilege, and wealth while others are subjected to inequities and discrimination (Christensen & Karp, 2003).

The reality of our nation's classrooms is that the teaching population remains largely White while the student population grows increasingly diverse. Therefore we must seek out various cultural resources in the school and community in order to understand and meet the needs of the students in our classrooms. As we consult with other teachers and community experts or bring parents and community members into the classroom, we can benefit from firsthand information about the values and differences represented in the cultures of our students.

Examining the degree of homelessness in different cultures and countries could serve to highlight the multicultural nature of the topic. Third-grade students could reflect on why homelessness is widespread in some parts of the world and why some impoverished cultures emphasize communal values in providing for those who do not have homes. Central to these explorations is the realization that people of color across the globe are more often homeless than those who are White. While this is a complex matter, students can begin to consider how race plays a role in who has power and is privileged in our world.

Social Justice Education Is Activist

Students can develop a deeper commitment to and understanding of working for social justice when they are presented with real opportunities to work for social justice in their lives. Taking action allows students to move from a position of powerlessness to one of possibility. In a social justice classroom, it is vital to provide students with opportunities to act in their schools and communities, to attempt to make concrete changes concerning issues that have been analyzed and critiqued in the classroom. We must encourage students to consider the wide range of possible actions that could make a difference, from working with individuals in the community to efforts aimed at changing public policies or laws. It is important that as teachers, we do not promote our own agendas or direct students to particular organizations or actions. Instead, we should help students analyze the issues, brainstorm options, and make choices as to what actions they would like to take.

The goal here is not charity or "do-gooding," which can potentially perpetuate racist, sexist, or classist assumptions when those who are "helping" are from the dominant culture and/or see themselves as somehow better than those who are in need. Ideally, students will work alongside those who have suffered from injustice for mutual support and empowerment. Yet, while we may encourage students to work for the rights of those who are dominated, marginalized, or excluded from society's benefits and opportunities, ultimately it is up to the students themselves to choose their issues of concern and the best-suited strategies for social change.

Informed by lessons learned in a unit on homelessness, third graders could brainstorm possible actions they might take to make a difference. These could range from indirect service (collecting food, clothing, or other needed items for a local shelter) to direct service (cooking and serving a meal at the local shelter, for example) to advocacy. Advocacy efforts could focus on writing letters to local newspapers or elected officials to inform them about homelessness and related issues and requesting legislators' assistance in passing laws or instituting policies that will provide jobs, low-income housing, disaster relief, and other needed services or programs.

CONCLUSION

A vision of social justice that embraces both the process of working toward a socially just world as well as a concrete image of that world is essential in social justice education. Focusing on the core themes of care and fairness, we can teach our students both for and about social justice as we build a socially just classroom community and learn about social issues in the world.

Effective social justice education in the elementary classroom is student-centered, collaborative, experiential, intellectual, critical, multicultural, and activist. These essential features can serve as guides for developing high-quality social justice curricula through which students practice socially just relating in the classroom and reach out to others as they work to create social justice in their communities and in the world.

Reflection Exercises

1. Consider the different views on the concept of social justice described in this chapter. In one paragraph, write your own personal definition of social justice.
2. Think about your education in schools from elementary school to the present and compare your experiences with the characteristics of quality social justice education. Can you identify teachers, lessons, or other school experiences that focused on one or more of these elements?
3. Outline a unit on a social justice issue of your choice, like the example in this chapter on homelessness, that incorporates the essential elements of social justice teaching.

3

Creating a Socially Just
Classroom Community

It's a lot more than the curriculum. In fact, in some ways I think it's
almost all more than the curriculum. It's how you treat those kids
with respect and empower them.

—Jane, Grades 5–6 teacher

Jane's assertion about the nature of social justice teaching brings to mind
the old adage, "Experience is a powerful teacher." Because children learn
so much from experience and by the examples we set in the classroom,
teaching for social justice must begin in the class community. It makes
no sense to teach lessons about social justice in U.S. history or engage
in activism in the local community if we are not also practicing social
justice in our relationships with each other in our classrooms. As fifth-
grade teacher Tessa noted, "It's the things you do day in and day out."
The classroom community offers a unique and important opportunity
to learn about social justice firsthand.

The classroom is the primary place in which children live and
work for many hours alongside others who are different from them.
In the typical elementary-school classroom, age is the only common
denominator. While some schools are more homogeneous than others
in regard to ethnicity and social class, every elementary school class
embodies the myriad of cultures, lifestyles, socioeconomic classes, religions, and intellectual and physical abilities present in the local community. One could hardly design a more ideal situation to practice
building and nurturing a socially just community.

However, *ideal* does not equal *easy*. Balancing the many demands
schools place on teachers with the individual needs of children is taxing.

And with the increasing stakes associated with state standards and tests, it can seem like there is little time to spend on relationship building.

Yet if we are serious about teaching for social justice this is exactly what we must do. As Jane noted in the opening of this chapter, teaching for social justice is as much—or more—about how we respect and empower the students in our classrooms as it is about social studies units or lessons. Fortunately, taking time to build a socially just and cohesive classroom community contributes to, rather than detracts from, students' academic learning. When students feel safe, supported, and valued, and when students begin to see themselves as competent and worthy of learning, their openness and ability to learn is enhanced (Nieto, 1999, p. 123). And when we encourage students to work together toward common goals on projects they care about, motivation to engage in learning increases.

The gem of a socially just classroom has many facets; respect, safety, trust, care, value, openness, courage, cooperation, and support are all essential. Where do we begin? And, given our limited time in the school day, what are the most effective strategies for actualizing these qualities in the classroom?

EMBRACING THE INDIVIDUAL

The bedrock of a socially just classroom is a climate of safety and trust in which each individual's unique strengths and needs are valued. As teachers, we can take the first steps toward establishing this foundation by meeting students' basic needs, treating them fairly and respectfully, valuing students' cultures, and creating a child-centered curriculum (e.g., learning activities that are relevant and interesting to children and allow them both voice and choice). While a socially just community supports and honors both the individual and the collective, we must begin with embracing every child's uniqueness and letting them know we value them for who they are, in all their wonder and confusion, with all their strengths and shortcomings, in their joys and in their sorrows.

Carmen, a kindergarten teacher in New York City, explains how she values both the individual and the group. "The way that I am in the world and the way that I see myself as a teacher was always making space for every individual in the group. . . . My idea was to not only have us be a group that could live well together, but also allow for the individual's voice and the individual presence to emerge."

There are many reasons to support Carmen's focus on the individual. We know that students have more difficulty learning if they are fearful, worried, or do not feel valued as individuals. And only when children are valued as individuals will they feel the necessary safety and support to engage in cooperative work with their peers to create a socially just classroom community, to work for social justice in the school and community, and to struggle through the inevitable conflicts that will arise in their work together. Without a sense of respect and trust, children will feel hesitant to speak up and reluctant to serve as allies for their peers. So part of our task is to embrace (rather than tolerate or bemoan) differences. In particular, it is vital that we visibly recognize and appreciate differences that others may disregard, avoid, or even criticize.

Seeing students as individuals and making accommodations for them based on their unique needs can make the difference for students who might otherwise be unsuccessful in school. Teaching for social justice embraces differences in ways that sometimes go beyond the typical elementary classroom. For example, we may choose to fully integrate children who are autistic or have other special needs. This may involve providing special learning experiences for a certain child or openly addressing with the class how they can all help to support students who need special accommodations to learn. Rather than treating everyone the same way according to the same rules, teaching for social justice involves recognizing differences and responding accordingly.

Part of the challenge in supporting individual needs is enlisting other students' support. Students may question why one child gets to sit in a chair when the rest of the students sit on the rug. Teaching for social justice involves not only making accommodations for individuals, but taking the time to explain to the rest of the class why these changes are necessary. We need to help children see that ultimately it is not about privilege or bending the rules, it is about providing every student with the experiences they need to reach their learning potential and be productive members of the class community.

Molly's second-grade class provides one example of how creating an accepting and inclusive classroom community sometimes involves exceptional support for one child. When a new Spanish-speaking student joined Molly's class one day, she sat him at a table with several other Spanish-speaking students. A girl in the class who spoke very little English herself took the new boy under her wing. With giggles and grins, she brought the Spanish books to their table, sat with him on the rug during story time, and showed him where the bathroom was. A Spanish lesson was planned for the day, a Friday morning ritual. Attendance, lunch count, and opening exercises in math were all conducted in Spanish. The students all sang the morning song to the tune of "Frère Jacques": *Buenos Días, Cómo Estás, Muy Bien Gracias, Y Usted.* "This is when the ESL students get a chance to shine," Molly noted. Later in the lesson, Señora Maria, the Spanish teacher, had all of the students show their self-portrait and introduce themselves in Spanish to the new student. The class responded with smiles and the Spanish greeting, *Hola.* What could have been a difficult first day for the student who spoke no English turned out to be a caring and fun lesson for all of the students on the importance of including every student in the community of the classroom.

As teachers, we play a critical role in the process of building a socially just classroom, yet we don't have the knowledge or power needed to do so alone. Students must buy into the challenge and lend their voices to the effort, as they willingly did in Molly's class. It is essential that we begin on the first day of school to create a climate in which students are encouraged to express their desires and concerns and to make choices about how they learn and play.

BUILDING A SOCIALLY JUST COMMUNITY FROM DAY ONE

Several strategies can prove especially helpful in these early stages of building a socially just community. Framing the focus on social justice with language that children can understand is an important first step. We can explain to students that we are all on equal ground no matter who we are, where we're from, what we can do, or what we can't do. We are all part of a family and we take care of each other. Even with the youngest children, we can make explicit our intentions to work together in creating a supportive and just class community. It's important to have group discussions in the beginning of the school year about community, what that means to us, and how we can work together.

Out of the ordinary events during the first week of school can help students realize the importance of the community building process. For example, students can build a "web" with a ball of yarn connecting them all to one another as a symbol of their interdependence and the need for teamwork. When one student tugs on the string they are holding, all are influenced by it. Lindsey, a sixth-grade teacher of children with emotional and behavioral disorders, begins her school year with a ritual using water that serves to bring the class together as a community.

> I have this big urn and I ask each of the children to bring in a cup of water from anywhere. It can be a stream, it can be the sink, it can be a water fountain. And I don't tell them what it's about. I send them a postcard in the summer before school starts, and they all come in with curiosity and wonder. What's this water for? . . . I talk about how we're going to build a community here, and I'd like each one of them to pour the water and tell us something about where their water came from and what they want to bring to the community and what they're hoping to receive from the community.

The water ritual is a visual representation of how we each can offer something of ourselves to create the whole of our classroom community. The ritual also serves to initiate the development of rules in this classroom. Following the ritual, students brainstorm guidelines they need to live and learn together as a class community and they come to consensus on a few rules that are posted and revisited throughout the year. Another strategy for student involvement in rule-making is having students place stickers next to the few rules from a brainstormed list that each thinks is important.

It is important in a social justice classroom to emphasize the positive and inclusive aspects of rules. Rather than rules like "No talking" or "Listen to the teacher," a social justice classroom might emphasize such rules as "Help your classmates," "Listen to everyone respectfully," and "State your opinions on issues that matter to you." We can even include rules that focus on working for social justice in the school and community such as "Help make the world a better place." Rules like this one teach children that our classroom community goes beyond how we relate to each other in the class. We are also part of our school and local community, and we have a responsibility to improve the small corner of our world where we see problems or potential.

Emphasizing student involvement in making class guidelines is vital for several reasons. If this is "our" class, they need to be "our" rules. Allowing for student voice and choice is evidence of our respect for children and our desire to empower children to speak up for what is important to them. When students participate wholeheartedly in the process of creating class guidelines, they are much more likely to value them, refer to them, and abide by them. Student voice is thus a critical aspect of an effective social justice classroom.

SPEAKING UP

While a traditional elementary classroom emphasizes students listening to the teacher and working quietly, social justice teaching calls attention to the students speaking up and contributing to the class community. In circle meetings, class discussions, and daily lessons, children are encouraged to express their opinions as well as to listen respectfully to others. While as teachers we must be mindful of curricular standards and district requirements, we can also place children's needs, interests, and desires at the forefront of our decisions about what and how they learn.

Jane expressed a strong opinion in this regard. "I don't want to have the power. I'm there to be the adult and to facilitate, but if all things are going well, I'm standing in a corner watching children talk to each other." Jane's teaching style emphasizes children's collaborative learning through discovery over the teacher's role as an instructor or purveyor of information. However, there is a balance to be maintained between fostering students' opinions, interests, and creativity, on the one hand, and recognizing that children need and want boundaries and limits, on the other. And while we know that children are individuals with varying needs, feelings, and interests; we also have an obligation—to our students, their families, and the educational system—to facilitate maximum learning for all of our students.

In traditional elementary classrooms children are primarily asked to listen to the teacher and to respond with the correct answers to teachers' questions. In a social justice–oriented classroom, it may take a while for students to realize that we really care about what they think and that we aren't just looking for the "right" answer. For very hesitant or quiet students, we may even provide instruction in how to speak up in front of a group. We can model or explain how to stand up straight, look at people's eyes, and project one's voice to the farthest person in the room. Students can practice these techniques with each other and in authentic public speaking experiences in other classrooms or at community meetings. We can support them by providing gentle reminders and encouragement as they learn to find their voices.

ARRANGING THE ROOM

Teaching for student voice and democratic participation is enhanced by how we structure the physical arrangement of our classrooms. Opportunities for sharing resources, working together on collaborative projects, and sitting in circles for discussion and problem solving are all important.

Social justice teaching will be facilitated by students sitting at tables or with their desks in small groups of four or six. This arrangement will aid group work and sharing resources. Rather than each child having an individual pencil or set of crayons, supplies can be assembled in cans or small boxes for the group as a whole to use. Supplies can be stored in the middle of the table or on a shelf in another part of the room. This arrangement helps to eliminate the problem of lost (borrowed? stolen?) supplies and also can ease the burden for children whose families cannot afford to contribute. And children will quickly realize that compiling their supplies has several advantages, including more crayon colors and a greater diversity of tools. This arrangement carries several powerful messages about social justice, not the least of which is that in caring for their supplies, children are responsible not only to themselves, but also to each other.

In order to foster effective learning and social relationships, assigned seats can be rotated or changed periodically with student input. Changing students' seats can help to deter the formation of cliques. It can also keep us as teachers from getting in ruts about who we call on or whose work we comment on during the day.

Every social justice classroom should provide space for students to sit in a circle, either on the floor or in chairs, to enable students to engage in face-to-face discussion and other types of circle meetings. The circle places everyone on the same level and allows everyone to hear and see anyone who is speaking. Sitting in circles has been and continues to be a familiar format for councils and group decision making in cultures across time and place.

SUPPORTING THE COMMUNITY WITH CIRCLE MEETINGS

Circle meetings—talking as a class while sitting on a rug, pillows, or chairs in a circle—serve a variety of purposes. Morning circle meetings are a time to check in with the children, renew a sense of class community, and review the upcoming schedule for the day. Circle meetings at the end of the school day can help to affirm good feelings and end the day on a positive note. And circle meetings at any time can be used to make class decisions or address the inevitable conflicts or problems that arise.

Stephanie, a fourth-grade teacher from Florida, includes a greeting in her morning circle meeting in which students can ask for a hug, a handshake, or a high five. Students have a choice as to the intimacy of their interaction, yet all three greetings build positive feelings in the group.

Circle meetings can also be held at the end of the week to give each child an opportunity to say something that they are proud of both about themselves and about a classmate before they leave for the weekend. Also held on Friday afternoons, a "Give or Get" circle helps young students end the week on a positive note by either giving a compliment to another student or saying "get" in order to receive a compliment from one's peers.

As students practice democracy in their class community, inevitably conflicts and problems arise. Circle meetings also prove useful for resolving problems. When I taught fourth grade in rural New Hampshire, the students met weekly to solve problems of their own choosing. Our social justice issues included the following problems: pencils being lost or stolen, boys teasingly spanking girls on the playground, and a conflict over whether wet socks or cold bodies should have priority for the classroom heater during the winter months. Often I noticed that when students just listened to their classmates' concerns, they found ways to resolve the problems without teacher intervention or punishments.

Mindful of the many demands placed on our time as teachers, Laurie alternates a friendship circle and a problem-solving circle on Wednesday afternoons each week. In the problem-solving circles, students write down issues, such as not sharing recess toys, which are then drawn from a box and discussed. Laurie learned about the friendship circle at a Quaker conference and adapted it for her fourth graders. "In the friendship circle what happens is that children will come to the circle with a feeling they will want to present to another child and they want to deal with it with the support of the class," stated Laurie. The choices are expressing anger toward someone, making an apology to a classmate, or thanking a peer. There are three signs that go with these options: stomping on the floor in front of the other student, shaking the other's hand, or bowing in front of the person, respectively. While the student receiving the expression has the option to say "no" for now and deal with the problem privately later on, Laurie contends that hardly ever do students choose to defer discussing the issue. "Most times it's just an individual thing and it gets resolved very quickly," noted Laurie. "Other times it comes out that it's a group issue, that a lot of children are angry at one child for the same thing. Then it becomes a class discussion. It's done in a mode so that the children don't feel attacked but do feel that they are hearing that something's not right and they had better focus on that."

Addressing conflict openly in this way gives students a powerful message about social justice: When we have difficulties in our community, we talk about them respectfully and attempt to resolve them so that everyone feels valued and appreciated and so everyone in our community enjoys each other. This may be a lofty goal with a group of 28 fourth graders, but it is an important effort that can teach them valuable life skills to apply to their personal lives and their civic involvement.

Circle meetings take time, yet if you consider the amount of time we spend as teachers managing student behavior and assisting with student conflicts, it is time well spent. In most elementary classrooms, circle meetings actually save time because they lessen the amount of conflict and problematic interactions among children. They also help children learn valuable social justice lessons. Through experiencing circle meetings, students come to recognize that living in a democratic society requires that we work hard to appreciate our differences, resolve our conflicts, and honor our varied perspectives as we attempt to make decisions that support the common good, as well as the needs of individuals.

WIDENING THE COMMUNITY

The strategies discussed so far will go a long way toward creating effective social justice classrooms in our schools. Yet we will be even more successful as teachers if we widen our communities to include parents, guardians, colleagues, and community members. Several scholars have noted that including parents and community members as partners in children's education increases teachers' effectiveness in the classroom (e.g., Ladson-Billings, 1994; Nieto, 2003; Rose, 1995). There are many ways we can welcome parents, guardians, and community members to engage with our students and contribute their expertise and ideas for the benefit of us all.

For example, outside of Molly's second-grade classroom, there is a large poster with photos of the children and their families, titled "Our Community—Partners in Learning." The photos were taken during Molly's home visits, an important part of her preparation for the new school year. During a 10-day period before the start of school, Molly goes to the homes of as many students as she can, learning about the children and their families. These visits build the foundation for connecting classroom learning with children's lives and including parents as frequent participants in the class.

As Molly's second graders transition from home to school in the morning, they put away their backpacks, sit at their tables in small groups, and begin silent reading. Parents linger to hug their sons and daughters, and several aides and special teachers come in to talk to Molly about working with some of her students during the day. Other classroom teachers and teacher education students from the local colleges are in and out of Molly's classroom throughout the day, collaborating with Molly and her students and contributing to the creation of her classroom as a vibrant and inclusive community.

We can also focus on building a wider community in the ways we support and share about children's learning with their families. Sending home newsletters to keep parents and guardians up-to-date with daily classroom events is important and can serve as a tool to invite their participation in the classroom. At Carmen's school, teachers send home progress reports twice a year that emphasize students' strengths. The long narrative letters are written to both children and their families so they can read and discuss them together.

Carmen and her colleagues also hold family conferences twice a year. Where typically a teacher would meet with just parents or guardians to review students' progress, family conferences place the child at the center of the discussion. Carmen explained, "It's a conversation about sharing about what their work has been, what their interests have been, what accomplishments they've made, and what things they're still working on." Family conferences help to meet many social justice teaching goals including empowering students to take ownership of their learning, to evaluate their learning, and to find their voices in speaking about themselves with their families and teachers.

TEACHING A SOCIAL CURRICULUM

Children learn valuable skills when they are included and encouraged to participate in family conferences and circle meetings. Learning from their experiences can be greatly enhanced when we teach an explicit social curriculum to our students as well. Several issues can be effectively addressed in the elementary classroom, including anger management, bullying, kindness, respect, empathy, self-esteem, and feelings. For example, Paula uses stuffed animals in her kindergarten class to help her students learn about peace building and conflict resolution. "Cool Cat" tells children not to lose their temper. A fluffy bunny and an angry alligator assist students in evaluating who makes a good friend.

Teaching about prejudice, stereotypes, and discrimination can help students learn about their own and others' challenges in creating a socially just world. Students can identify stereotypes related to gender, ethnicity, class, religion, or other factors in children's literature, the media, and everyday conversation on the playground or in the supermarket. As children are very concerned with fairness, they will quickly learn to recognize stereotypes in the language and actions of those around them and will be able to point out many examples in the popular media. After students become aware of stereotypes, we can teach them ways to try to change their own and others' thinking. Effective strategies include how to talk to others respectfully when one notices a stereotype being promoted and how to work for change through civic and political avenues.

PUTTING IT ALL TOGETHER: MELINDA'S "KIDS WHO CARE" CLASS

Powerful learning results when we not only teach a social curriculum but also practice social justice in our classroom relationships and community building. Melinda, a third-grade teacher, uses several strategies to create a socially just classroom community.

While the task of creating a socially just society may seem daunting and even unobtainable at times, Melinda finds her class of 8-year-olds a perfect opportunity to work toward creating a socially just community on a small scale. A Lebanese American woman who is active locally in antidiscrimination efforts, she is no stranger to the issue of social injustice, especially since 9/11, after which a parent called the principal to say, "You have an Arab American at your school. Is that a conflict of interest?" Due to her personal experience and community activism, Melinda has a perspective on the nature of social justice that openly addresses issues of power and oppression. As she says, "The beauty about teaching elementary school is that you can teach social justice as the curriculum and you can build a culture of social justice in your classroom so that you can see injustice and call it as it happens in your daily life."

"The circle area of our classroom is very important," Melinda says. "I bring them to the circle and they sit in the circle all year whenever we're learning something new or having a discussion because it's a place of equality with no one higher." Melinda emphasizes two key points to her third graders during the first days of school: that the classroom is a place where students can make mistakes and learn from them and that she wants to work with the students to create a classroom of "kids who care." Melinda defines *"kids who care"* as "kids who care about themselves, care about each other, care about people in the world, and care about the environment."

Melinda's class spends part of every day during the first few weeks of school making lists about how kids who care can expect to be treated and how they treat others. These lists evolve into a class constitution. Melinda guides her third graders in "making some basic commitments to each other so that when any of us sees behavior that feels unfair or unjust or uncaring, it's not a harsh discipline." Instead of implementing a strict system of punishments or consequences, Melinda chooses to remind her students of how to be caring to each other. For example, in response to a child who grabs another student's markers, Melinda might say, "We decided as a class that kids who care ask instead of grab." Melinda applies this strategy to playground conflicts, aggressive acts, and situations that call for problem solving as well. Melinda takes a consistent, persistent, and patient approach to building her classroom community.

But do her students buy in to the kids-who-care philosophy and language? "They do," asserted Melinda, "because eventually they start saying it to each other when somebody grabs or when somebody causes an accident or when somebody runs past them or cuts in front of them. They say 'kids who care say excuse me, you know.'" When Melinda had a new student join the class in January, she asked the students to introduce themselves and tell the new student something about their classroom. Melinda was surprised when her students said things like "This is a class where nobody puts another person down" or "We all work really hard on being kids who care." The fact that students' words were unprompted by their teacher evidences their ownership of the kids-who-care concept. The students wanted to make the new child feel welcome and also let her know that there was an expected standard of relating in their classroom.

In addition to building a socially just classroom community, Melinda, along with her colleague Bruce, teaches lessons on stereotyping. The students look at images in the media and analyze the messages they are getting, deciding which messages they think are true and which are not. "We start with groups," noted Melinda. "Who are the people you've heard stereotypes about? And of course this year, they talked about Arabs and Muslims." Melinda asked her students to bring in images of people they thought were Arab or Muslim, and they made lists of the things they had heard and what they wanted to find out about. This activity led to students' exploration of stereotypes of many groups. They laid out all of the images, categorized them, and then critically assessed whether their views of the images were positive, negative, or just neutral observations.

Melinda, Bruce, and a third teacher in their school wrote a literature-based social competency curriculum for their students focused on conflict resolution. They began by having students examine conflict individually within their real-life experiences and then asked students to parallel those experiences with characters they read about. The students then discussed ways to resolve the conflicts, both in real life and in the children's literature books. The curriculum the teachers created is based on the Open Circle program at Wellesley College. Open Circle (http://www.open-circle.org) is a program that helps elementary schools create a sense of classroom community and provide a forum for children to learn practical social and emotional skills.

Melinda connects the curriculum to her classroom community by asking her students how kids who care solve their conflicts with each other. She asks her students to explore the roles people can play in a conflict. "There are teasers and bullies, there are bystanders and targets," Melinda explained. She tries to help her students understand the many reasons why a child might tease or bully another and how one can work to change something with the help of allies. She recognizes that this is social justice work that may not pay off immediately. "The hope is," she says, "that we're building a new culture for the future."

Melinda's teaching illustrates how powerful teaching for social justice coheres through several mutually supportive strategies. Through circle meetings, creating a class constitution, teaching a comprehensive social curriculum, and persistent positive reinforcement, Melinda and her third graders developed a class community characterized by safety, kindness, and student ownership.

CONCLUSION

Teaching for social justice is much more than topics or lessons in the social studies curriculum. From room arrangement to strategies that support student voice and choice, the process of relating respectfully to our students and building a supportive class community provides students with direct experience that translates to powerful lessons on the nature and practice of social justice. Empowering students within an inclusive community that embraces differences, welcomes parents, and collaborates with school colleagues, we can model democratic living on a small scale, giving our students firsthand skills in practicing relating in a socially just way each and every day.

Reflection Exercises

1. Develop a plan for creating a socially just classroom community at the beginning of the school year for a grade level of your choice. Consider the

room arrangement, development of class rules or guidelines, and an activity for the first day that emphasizes the type of community you hope to create with your students.

2. Write a one-page essay in response to the following questions: What are the advantages and disadvantages to having circle meetings in an elementary classroom? What strategies and behavior management techniques might facilitate the effective use of circle meetings? How might you use circle meetings in your classroom?

3. Review the ideas in this chapter and write down at least five beliefs students might learn about themselves from being part of a socially just classroom community. For example, students who practice speaking in public might come to believe that "I have important ideas." For each belief, be prepared to discuss how it might contribute to positive civic identity and participation.

4

Reinventing the Social
Studies Curriculum

Why are we always teaching about wars? If you want to change things
then you focus on what you think is important, like movements and
things that people have done to change the world in a good way, not
wars.

—Kara, Grade 2 teacher

Teaching social studies for social justice requires taking a fresh look at
the standard topics taught at the elementary level. As Kara points out
in the quote above, if we aim to promote social justice in our classrooms
and in the world, we need to look critically at the topics we choose to
teach. This chapter is concerned with how to effectively choose social
studies content for social justice goals. Given our standards and test-
driven educational environment, this effort requires a willingness to
"think outside the box" and to be creative in our approach to curriculum development.

Social studies in the elementary school has always been, and likely
always will be, a curricular smorgasbord. From ancient Rome to contemporary global issues, topics in social studies education bridge time
and space to introduce children to learning about their world. Drawing primarily on seven social sciences (history, psychology, sociology,
anthropology, economics, geography, and political science), social
studies is the study of the world's people—their history, cultures, and
interactions.

What could possibly be more fascinating than studying humanity?
With our varied lifestyles and values across the globe and throughout
history, social studies draws on an intriguing and rich array of cultures,

31

historical events, and geographic diversity. And besides being interesting, social studies is also of critical importance in our problem-ridden democratic society. The professed mission of social studies is to educate our youth to become informed and active citizens of our multicultural nation and world.

Yet despite its potential, social studies is the most marginalized subject in the elementary school curriculum (Houser, 1995). Several factors account for this situation. First, literacy and mathematics are deemed the subjects most useful in the work world and most likely to increase America's domination in the global market; thus the priority in time, materials, and training is usually accorded to those two subjects. Second, districts tend to emphasize subjects assessed in high-stakes testing, and not many states include social studies in this effort (Houser, 1995). With few resources, little time, and less importance allocated to social studies, instruction typically focuses on the textbook, which students find boring and monotonous.

For more than a century, social studies instruction in the United States has primarily followed what is called the expanding environments or expanding horizons sequence (K—self, 1—family, 2—neighborhood, 3—community, 4—state, 5—nation, 6—Canada and Mexico). This model, developed by Paul Hanna at the turn of the twentieth century, is based on the idea that as students mature, they are increasingly exposed to wider aspects of the world, and can then study them successfully (Akenson, 1987). However, Hanna could not foresee the development of the global marketplace and our technological connections that have resulted in students being exposed at very young ages to people and places far beyond their own neighborhoods. Nor could Hanna predict that our society would become increasingly multicultural or that researchers would discover that young children have far greater capacities for learning about facts and ideas beyond their immediate surroundings than originally thought (Levstik & Barton, 2005).

All of these developments have led many social studies educators and scholars to question the relevance of the expanding horizons model for the twenty-first century. And if we add to these facts on the state of elementary social studies the staggering poverty, illness, and environmental degradation on the planet, clearly a new approach to social studies is not only wise, it is also a hopeful and necessary means for responding to a world and its people in crisis.

Teaching about social justice places social studies front and center in the curriculum. Social studies is especially well suited to teaching about the oppressive tendencies and antioppressive possibilities of individuals, cultures, institutions, and histories (Kumashiro, 2004). With creativity, we can adapt or change the standard curriculum and still meet the requirements of our districts and states, both in social studies and in other curricular areas as well.

ADAPTING THE STANDARD CURRICULUM

While the standard curriculum topics are not especially oriented toward social justice goals, they are usually broad themes that can be taken in different directions. For example, the third-grade curriculum on community could include a unit on homelessness and a first-grade family curriculum could emphasize the diversity of families (e.g., blended, biracial, intergenerational, or gay) and ask students to consider if all families are treated fairly and equally in the community.

Economics is one of the third-grade social studies standards in Kara's school. "What some of the third grades do is teach a lot about money and about supply and demand; and they will maybe set up a store or a garage sale and have kids sell for profit," explained Kara. "I dealt with the economic standard through the child labor unit." Thus Kara teaches the same economic principles as her colleagues, yet she is able to teach her students valuable social justice lessons as well.

A typical sixth-grade focus is ancient civilizations: Egypt, Greece, China, and so forth. With a focus on what we can learn from early civilizations, their lifestyles, their struggles, how they organized their society, and how they lived together in community, we can glean ideas that may be useful in creating a socially just society today. We can also look at current events connected with the history of ancient civilizations (for example, the war in Iraq), thus creating further social justice connections.

It is also helpful if we focus on the concepts and principles central to a topic, rather than dates and isolated facts. For example, in teaching a unit on explorers, we can focus on issues around the use of power and oppression. Molly explained how she breaks down these complex social justice concepts for her second graders.

We talk about the difference between exploration and invasion. We talk about it in terms of your house. Someone can visit your house and that would be different than if someone invaded your house. Someone came and didn't go and they pushed you out the back door and took all your toys. That's not exploration, that's invasion. I know that they know the difference between visit, explore, conquer, invade, occupy.

Molly concluded,

They understand those things, and I think that's more important than knowing what year Balboa set foot on this little peak in the Pacific.

All of these examples provide evidence that social studies topics with seemingly little connection to social justice can, with some creativity, be taught from a social justice perspective. Choosing specific aspects of broad topics, connecting historical topics to present-day concerns, and teaching the essential principles of a topic rather than isolated facts are three effective strategies for transforming traditional social studies content.

But are there some social studies themes that cannot be adapted to teach for a social justice perspective? While it might be possible to modify any topic to incorporate social justice goals, some themes and curriculum materials seem to make the task almost insurmountable. From developmentally inappropriate topics to scripted teacher's guides, we may feel frustrated with and resistant to some of the required curricula. "It's ridiculous, can you believe this?" questioned Kris. "Second grade, we're supposed to be teaching the War of 1812. I've never heard of anything so stupid. . . . In an ideal world, I think that a lot of the topics would arise from what the kids are interested in." Each of us must make thoughtful choices about the degree to which we resist teaching required curricular topics. In some cases, we are required to teach what we may deem to be irrelevant topics, but hopefully we can spend minimal time on these aspects of the curriculum.

Social studies textbooks are more often than not a deterrent in our efforts to teach meaningful content for social justice goals. Opening any given chapter of a social studies textbook, one may find a page that deals with slavery and the next page on a specific colony, glossing over each topic with a few sentences and an illustration or two. Many textbooks seem to assemble almost random bits of information, without much controversy and from limited cultural perspectives. Teaching for social justice requires going above and beyond the textbook to seek out resources within the school and community that enliven the curriculum and bring meaningful social justice content to classroom lessons.

While we can think outside the box and be creative in transforming the social studies curriculum, in reality, most of us also make at least a few concessions to the prevailing norms. When Saphira moved to a new school, the other kindergarten teachers expected her to teach the same curriculum that they had planned. She refused to teach "the cute little bears" unit, but she did agree "to let the nature lady come in January." "She came and did her thing, but it didn't fit what I was doing," Saphira noted. "I tried to do some things their way, because I didn't want to make too many waves. I'm already making big waves anyway." Saphira, like most of us, has to weigh and choose the options of when to teach for social justice and when to go along with the traditional norms for teaching and learning in her school.

Effective teaching for social justice, especially within a traditional school setting, is a balancing act that involves creative adaptation, thoughtful resistance, and compromise. How we juggle these responses to the curriculum depends as much, if not more, on personal conviction and perseverance than on district mandates. Teaching for social justice involves working from a sense of our own commitment and efficacy as decision makers and change agents.

DEALING WITH STANDARDS AND TESTS

The influence of district- and state-mandated standards and tests on our work may provide another source of frustration or challenge, as it does for many teachers nationwide, both in social studies (Grant, 1997) and, indeed, in all subject areas (Gratz, 2000). Sometimes what we need to do to meet state standards or prepare our students for statewide tests can limit our time for social justice teaching. The goals for statewide accountability in our educational systems can even seem opposed to our efforts to teach social justice topics and skills. Learning to question the status quo and developing the skills necessary to become an effective change agent are not usually the featured goals in social studies state tests. And even when the content of state tests appears to be important learning, it may not match what is needed or desired by a particular group of children. Echoing this mismatch, Amy asked, "Where's the balance between mandating stuff that you know is good practice and giving opportunities for child-centered learning and for the kinds of things that come out of the needs of the community and the school and the parents working together?"

In response to the frustration that can be engendered when attempting to teach for social justice in a standards-based environment, we may need to use creative and even subversive teaching methods. Herbert Kohl, noted progressive educator and author, described this type of teaching as "creative maladjustment."

> It implies adapting your own particular maladjustment to the nature of the social systems that you find repressive. It also implies learning how other people are affected by those systems, how personal discontent can be appropriately turned into moral and political action. (Kohl, 1994a, p. 130)

We can practice creative maladjustment in response to standardized testing. Some of us may choose to resist these tests. Others of us may decide to resist teaching to the test but to spend some time teaching students how to take the tests because of the impact that test scores will have on students' lives.

Most states now have state standards for social studies that require certain topics to be taught at specified grade levels. Again, the mismatch between these standards and social justice teaching provides opportunities to practice creative maladjustment. We can choose broad themes, such as civil rights or human rights, and then fit our social justice activities under the social studies standards. We may also be able to meet other standards in reading and writing at the same time when using an integrated approach to instruction. Or we can develop our social justice curriculum first, and then look for and find some support in the state standards. An additional strategy is to take an activist approach and get involved in helping to write local or state standards, thus working to create a degree of alignment between one's social justice values and goals and the required curriculum.

Yet even in the face of district mandates and state standards, many of us can close the classroom door and teach what we want, at least for part of the day. When teaching for social justice is important to us and we aren't being overly scrutinized by the administration, we can take greater latitude in shaping a meaningful and exciting social studies curriculum.

TEACHING HISTORY FOR SOCIAL JUSTICE

History, especially U.S. history, plays a central role in the elementary social studies curriculum and is traditionally taught with a focus on dates and facts about presidents and wars. The early history of the United States (e.g., Native Americans, explorers, pioneers) is taught at many grade levels in the elementary school. Typically, a large segment of the fourth-grade curriculum centers on one's state history and in the fifth grade, U.S. history is the focus for the entire year.

Thus it is important to consider how we can teach history for social justice aims. Earlier in this chapter, I discussed connecting historical content to contemporary social justice issues and teaching the central principles and concepts of historical events, rather than isolated and unimportant facts. Another effective strategy is to study the "people's history" rather than the history of the wealthy and famous. Studying grassroots movements for the rights of workers, women, cultural groups, and people with disabilities can help our students learn about our country's legacy in working for social justice. Seren, a teacher in the Bronx, takes this approach with his second and third graders.

> The whole idea of social history rather than political history and the ways it happens in college classes can really be brought into elementary school in talking about not just wars and kings, but about what real people were doing at any given time and how real people lived.

And when teaching about "real people" don't forget to include children. Elementary students are fascinated with studying the games, schooling, and family life of children from the past. Much of this content has social justice connections. The history of child laborers in this country, for example, raises important questions about fairness and caring in regard to the treatment of young people, and we can find many examples of children in history who worked for social change.

History teaching provides an excellent opportunity for looking at the legacy of injustice in the world as well. Peter, a fifth-grade teacher in Chicago, takes a strong social justice stance by focusing on issues of power, domination, and abuse throughout his history teaching.

> We boiled it down to how the concepts of "we" and "they" are shown throughout history and what have been the ramifications of that, with the power elite and the people who don't have power. How has human history gone forward from that, through warfare and through intolerance and justification of killing hundreds and thousands and millions of people?

Peter's willingness to highlight injustice in history opens up many possibilities for his students' learning. Studying injustice can increase students' awareness, empathy, and even moral outrage, hopefully motivating students to care about others and to work for social justice.

An essential aspect of social justice education is considering multiple perspectives, and history teaching presents an excellent opportunity for looking at the differing views and values of people who lived in the past. Teaching multiple perspectives can help students realize that there is more than one story that can be told about any event that happens. For example, we can study Columbus's voyage to the Americas from the European and Native American perspectives, thus giving students very different impressions of this influential event in our nation's history. Students can discuss or write responses to the following questions: Why do we have a day off school to celebrate Columbus? Was he a hero, a criminal, or both? Teaching about how Columbus and his fellow explorers treated the native peoples they encountered raises serious social justice issues that can also be applied to the encounters between people of different cultures today.

With creativity, we can teach history in our elementary classrooms and maintain a central focus on social justice. We can teach the history of ordinary people's efforts to work for social justice through grassroots movements. At the same time, we can focus on multiple perspectives and highlight issues of power, oppression, and injustice, as well as connect history to contemporary social justice issues in current events. All of these strategies can work together to assist us in effectively teaching history for social justice goals.

SEEKING SUPPORT FOR SOCIAL JUSTICE TEACHING

Challenging prevailing norms and practices to reinvent the social studies curriculum isn't easy. While our inner conviction that we are "doing the right thing" can carry us a long way, we will also benefit from seeking out other sources of support to sustain our social justice teaching.

Colleagues

Many of us look to our colleagues for support, especially those who share a commitment to social justice teaching. However, some of us may not be able to identify a colleague in our school with similar values. Laurie, a teacher in inner-city Philadelphia, asserted that "finding an ally is really kind of like finding a pea under the mattress." Another teacher spoke about being seen as "elitist" and "feeling like an outsider" because she hadn't gone to the same local high school and college as many of her colleagues. Several teachers emphasized that they felt pressured to prove themselves as "good teachers" (translated as having students achieve academically) because they were teaching differently from their colleagues.

Even if you feel like you are the sole champion for social justice in your school, there are creative and assertive ways to reach out to your colleagues and develop a more supportive work environment. Posting student work in the hallway to initiate discussion and setting up book clubs or teacher autobiography sharing in the evening at each other's homes are two possibilities. Sometimes the best thing to do is to talk to the people who are against social justice teaching and to seek to understand their perspectives. At other times, it may be best to work quietly in your classroom and collaborate on the less controversial aspects of your curriculum. If your social justice teaching is effective, students will be your best advocates. As they move on to other classrooms, they will likely share their enthusiasm for what they learned under your care and ask for additional opportunities to express their views, learn from multiple perspectives, and make a difference in their school and community.

Parents

Parents can play an important role as supporters of our work. When children are excited about school, parents are generally supportive. Amy, in explaining why she has been able to teach for social justice, asserted, "Parents have infinitely more power than teachers do when it comes to what we do in our classrooms. . . . If they support you, you can get away with all kinds of subversive activity."

Of course, interactions with parents can also be difficult at times. Kara had a parent who did not want her child to participate in some of the class activities on civil rights, because she worried that her daughter would be too upset. And if our values are not the same as our students' families, we may need to prove ourselves to be "good" teachers. In general, however, parents are very supportive of social justice teaching because they recognize the benefits to their children in terms of personal empowerment, caring for others, and working for positive change in the community.

It is helpful to begin building support among parents even before the beginning of the school year with home visits or letters. Arranging to visit students' homes before school begins is well worth the investment of time. Home visits place teachers and families on a more nearly level playing field and help everyone begin to get to know one another. As teachers, we can gain a bit of insight into how our students' families function and relate with each other. We can also learn about the family's culture, interests, and expectations for their child in the upcoming school year. Most important, home visits are the first step in creating a trusting relationship that can be further developed as we work with families throughout the school year to provide children with the best possible education.

School Culture

Some of us are lucky enough to work in a school whose mission, climate, and curriculum support teaching social studies for social justice. If this is your situation, I hope you appreciate the unique nature of your workplace and the fit between the school's curriculum standards and your social justice goals. Gaia teaches at an alternative public school whose vision is "an active family of students, staff, parents, and neighbors, which values diversity and creativity, generates enthusiasm for lifelong learning, and nurtures humane, environmentally conscious, strong global citizens." When Gaia teaches social justice lessons, she can reference her school's mission statement and count on the support of her colleagues and principal.

Not surprisingly, elementary schools with an expressed social justice focus are most often found in progressive university towns or large urban areas with extensive multicultural populations. These schools cohere around mission statements and guidelines that embrace social justice and are often structured as democratic environments where teachers make many collective decisions about the curriculum and other school matters.

In schools and communities with little expressed emphasis on social justice, we must work harder to create a school climate supportive of social justice. While this effort can be initiated through networking with other like-minded teachers, building a schoolwide culture for social justice teaching will be more effective if top-down efforts are also initiated. Actions such as developing a social justice–oriented mission statement, gaining support from the principal or PTA, setting up special in-service sessions, and adopting social justice–oriented curriculum materials can all help to promote a focus on social justice teaching among many of the staff in your school.

Networking Beyond the School

Whether you teach in a social justice–oriented school or find that local support of any type for your social justice teaching is lacking, consider seeking meaningful connections through one of several national organizations of social justice teachers. Rethinking Schools, Teaching for Change, Educators for Social Responsibility, Radical Teacher, and the Teaching Tolerance program at the Southern Poverty Law Center all provide curricula and workshops or conferences to support teaching for social justice. (See Appendix A for the Web site addresses of these organizations). You might also find support in regional or statewide educational organizations. In addition, many colleges and universities offer courses on social justice–related themes; inquire especially within colleges of education for courses on social justice education or multicultural issues.

SOCIAL JUSTICE TEACHING IN ACTION

The following descriptions of teaching illustrate how three teachers creatively structured their social studies curriculum to incorporate many of the essential characteristics of social justice education discussed in Chapter 1. The first two teachers are working in schools that encourage their social justice teaching. Rob has a fifth-grade classroom in an inner-city school, Rebecca teaches a third-grade class in a rural university community. In the third description, Laurie's fourth-grade experience illustrates how a teacher in an unsupportive environment creates meaningful opportunities to teach for social justice.

Questioning History: Rob's Fifth Grade

Rob teaches in a midwestern inner-city school where instructional practices focus on cooperative learning, whole language instruction, democratic discipline, and critical thinking. Rob and his colleagues use a child-centered, hands-on approach to teaching that includes student projects, portfolio assessment, and strong parental involvement in students' education and school decision making. The following school themes guide instruction in social studies as well as all other school subjects:

1. We respect ourselves and our world.
2. We send messages when we communicate.
3. We can make a difference on planet Earth.
4. We share stories of the world.

Rob places special emphasis on social justice issues in teaching social studies:

> Throughout the year we talk about the fact that there's been historically movements for social justice in our world, in our nation, and we examine those. . . . We talk about how there's currently movements for social justice in our world and we look at those and current events. . . . Then I talk about how there will continue to be movements for social justice in the future. . . . I talk about how I'm involved in those movements . . . and that they will have to make the decision in the future. Every person makes a decision, consciously or unconsciously, whether or not they're involved in movements for social justice.

The following classroom vignette illustrates how student interest, critical thinking, and activism are integrated in Rob's teaching:

We were discussing the American Revolution and I had talked about how George Washington was a slave owner . . . and then somebody said, "Well, how many presidents did own slaves?" And I said, "Well, I don't actually know that. I know that Thomas Jefferson did and that Andrew Jackson did, but let's try to find out."

So the students and Rob searched the Internet and eventually found that 18 presidents owned slaves at some point. They made bar graphs and pie charts about who owned slaves and the number of years that slave owners ruled the country. "Interestingly enough," Rob noted, "up to the Civil War, the only people who had 8-year terms for president were slave owners."

Then Rob had his students divide up the 18 presidents and look them up in the history textbook to see what they could find. "The district had just adopted a spanking new textbook with all the bells and whistles and stuff, and so we looked in that and of course there was not one mention of a president owning slaves," Rob noted.

Some of the students ended up writing a letter of complaint to the textbook publisher. They received an "unapologetic" response saying that there is a lot of information about the presidents and they can't include everything in a textbook. Rob noted that there were several results of this lesson:

One is that kids developed a sense that they can't trust texts very much. . . . I think by looking for information on so many people and finding it so inadequate, that lesson was driven home. Another thing is that kids had a sense that they could try to do something about it, which was to write a letter. . . . Plus, the kids learned something about U.S. history. . . . That's an example of a lesson that was unplanned—came from a kid really—it just evolved and emerged and it was great.

Rob concluded with some thoughts on the challenge of teaching social justice to elementary students:

Social justice movements are not easy. People are. Martin Luther King Jr., Rosa Parks, there are various people who fought for social justice. The idea of kids, especially at this age level, understanding organizing and the need for organization and strategy and so on, it's partial understanding, but it's partial understanding for most adults. So I make an effort to relate the big movements for social justice throughout the year to various things so kids can get a sense of that.

Rob's lessons on the presidents are not what an elementary teacher would typically cover; they provide an apt illustration of how we can adapt a topic from the traditional curriculum to teach social justice content and skills.

Literature-Based Activism: Rebecca's Third Grade

For several reasons, Rebecca's third-grade classroom is an ideal place to teach for social justice. With only 14 students in her class, the group seems more like a family, especially given that there are two pairs of twins and one set of triplets among them. With the exception of math, Rebecca is free to design her own curriculum. Also, all teachers at Rebecca's school are *expected* to teach about social justice and involve their students in civic action. This is due to the fact that the school has been designated a First Amendment School, one of several nationwide whose mission is to teach about the First Amendment. The First Amendment, passed in 1791, states:

> Congress shall make no law respecting an establishment of religion, or prohibiting the free exercise thereof; or abridging the freedom of speech, or of the press; or the right of the people peaceably to assemble, and to petition the government for a redress of grievances.

First Amendment Schools must do more than teach children facts and principles; they are required to engage students in meaningful civic contributions to their school and community.

> First Amendment rights are best guarded and civic responsibilities best exercised when citizens are actively engaged in building a more just and free society. . . . Learning about freedom and justice, however important, can never be enough; educating for democratic citizenship must be more than an academic exercise. If we are to sustain and expand the American experiment in liberty, young citizens must acquire the civic skills and

virtues needed to exercise their freedom with responsibility. (Haynes, Chaltain, Ferguson, Hudson, & Thomas, 2003, pp. 20–21)

Inquiring About Religious Freedom

At the beginning of the school year, Rebecca's third graders studied the clauses about freedom of religion in the First Amendment, a challenging task for 8-year-olds. Then they watched a video about the many Jewish families who immigrated to the United States from Russia and Europe seeking freedom of religion, especially after World War II. Students read several books by Patricia Polacco including *The Keeping Quilt* (about a quilt passed down in a Jewish family for babies, weddings, and holy day celebrations), *Mrs. Katz and Tush* (about a friendship between an African American boy and an elderly Jewish woman), and *Chicken Sunday* (highlighting the African American culture and the observance of Easter). In addition to the religious freedom theme, students discussed the relationships between the young people and the older adults and issues of diversity presented in the books.

Next, Rebecca asked her students to consider, "What do you think would happen if people did not have freedom of religion?" Reading the book *Butterfly* by Patricia Polacco guided students in answering that question. The book is based on the author's family history; Polacco's aunt helped Jewish people escape to freedom from the Nazi regime. This book helped the students to understand that it is important to protect the religious freedom of others.

Learning about how one student in the class celebrates the Islamic month of Ramadan gave the third graders a concrete experience in understanding religious freedom. Since Ramadan is observed in remembrance of those who are poor, Rebecca guided the students in brainstorming what they could do to help others. Following a brainstorming session, the students filled out a worksheet in small groups titled "Looking through the lens of social action." The directions stated: "Look over and think about the lists of social concerns and needs that our class came up with. Select the THREE you believe are most important to work together on to create social action plans to address the concerns."

Students' written responses included, "Giving money to orfiniges" [orphanages], "pen pal with other kids less forcunet" [fortunate], and "giving things to the victoms [victims] of the hurricane rita." After working in small groups, the students put their ideas on chart paper and looked at the ideas to try to identify their commonalities. The common ideas were "help the poor" and "help the hungry." Based on this focus, students worked on helping the victims of Hurricane Rita.

Rebecca was also able to make use of the butterfly theme from the *Butterfly* book by Polacco in other subject lessons. In art, students created a model of the monarch butterfly that represented freedom to the Jewish child in the book. Students studied the parts of the monarch butterfly in science.

Contributing to the School Community

Helping to create and maintain a butterfly garden on the school grounds gave Rebecca's third graders an opportunity to use their new knowledge to contribute to their school community. First, students researched and wrote reports on butterflies. The students learned which flowers would attract butterflies, how best to arrange the plants, and how to create a water source for the butterflies to sip. This information was shared with a health and leisure studies professor from the local university who would oversee the planting. Then one Friday the professor presented information on planting the bushes and flowers. The students were divided into four groups with specific tasks: Air group—loosen the soil; Special group—put bushes in ground; Food group—give plants fertilizer; Water group—water the plants.

On Monday morning, Rebecca returned her students' attention to the butterfly garden project. She began, "We're going to talk about what we did with our butterfly garden. First thing, why did we make a butterfly garden? What was the purpose of it?" Rebecca constructed a web on the blackboard as students offered ideas such as "attract insects," "make the world more beautiful," and "went with butterfly unit."

Rebecca asked her class to consider how they could educate younger students in the school about the butterfly garden and the importance of taking care of it. After some negotiation, half of the students went to the back rug to discuss their ideas while the other half took a few minutes to write down their ideas at their desks. When the two groups reconvened, a lively discussion with many ideas ensued. One boy proposed they make signs to protect the butterfly garden; several students debated whether the kindergarteners would be able to read the signs, what words they can read and can't. "Maybe we can make pictures," stated one student. "Maybe we can teach them to read the signs," offered another. Another idea proposed was to "stay outside for an extra 5 or 10 minutes, use up all our recess time to guard the plants, and then we would get our recess time after they go back in." Students also suggested going to the K–2 classrooms to share about the garden and making a fence.

As the discussion wound down, Rebecca made an observation that helped organize the students' next steps toward civic action. Rebecca noted their ideas generally fit in one of three categories: making signs for the garden, going to the classrooms to explain, and having someone be outside to stand next to the garden to tell others not to hurt the garden. Rebecca asked her students to each choose one of these three ideas and form a group to work out a plan.

Rebecca took the two students who chose protecting the garden during recess to the back table and asked them to talk about what they planned to say. "Are we the only kids who picked this?" they asked. They seem surprised and a bit dismayed. "I don't want to spend my whole recess guarding the garden. I want to go on the swings," admitted one boy. Rebecca encouraged them to be positive in their interactions with the primary students. "Tell them what to do, show them what to do," she told the boys. One boy had the idea to allow the younger students to be helpers, and Rebecca praised this idea. She also reminded them that if the younger children don't listen to them, they can always go to the adult aides on the playground.

After each group had time to work on their plans, Rebecca reconvened the class and asked them to share their plans with each other. After each presentation, Rebecca asked, "Any comments about what they said? Any positive comments?" A few students affirmed their classmates' ideas. Rebecca concluded the lesson by telling the students, "You had a lot of great ideas!"

When students arrived at school the next morning, Rebecca showed them how she had organized their ideas in a chart on the blackboard. "These are your ideas that you gave yesterday," she observed. "I just gave the topic sentence." Listed on the board were the following sentences:

I. Purpose: The butterfly garden serves many purposes.
   A. Make the world more beautiful.
   B. Invite, attract insects.
   C. Add plants and color to the playground.
   D. Help monarch butterflies.

      E. Help Unit II learn about insects.

      F. Give the playground something special.

  II. There are many ways to take care of the butterfly garden.

     Students continued to work on the ideas in their groups from Monday (making signs, going to classrooms to teach children about the garden, and protecting the garden during recess). Rebecca encouraged the class to make decisions associated with the classroom presentations. "We have eight people to go to four classrooms. What would be a fair way to decide who goes to each class?" she asked. Several ideas were offered, including the one enacted, to put the eight students' names in a hat to draw.

     Several aspects of effective social justice teaching are evident in the few lessons from Rebecca's classroom recounted here. Throughout the activities, student voice is encouraged and respected. Students are empowered to share and receive affirmation for their ideas, to build on each other's ideas, and to put their ideas into action. Students are also frequently asked to reflect on their learning and apply classroom knowledge to their efforts as civic participants. These lessons illustrate how teachers can effectively combine social skills training with integrated, thematic teaching. In regard to the list of social justice education characteristics in Chapter 1, Rebecca's teaching is student-centered, collaborative, experiential, intellectual, and activist.

Learning from Another Child's Activism

Rebecca modeled the remaining two characteristics from the list— multicultural and critical—in another set of lessons. She read a book to the class, *Save My Rainforest* by Monica Zak, about an 8-year-old boy in Mexico who campaigns to save the rain forest. Rebecca told the children that they too could take action the way the boy in Mexico did. After reading aloud a note from the author in the back of the book, Rebecca asked, "What can you learn from this young man? What can we learn from his message and his story?"

     The students' answers reveal important insights for youth engaged in social change. "I learned that you don't have to do everything by yourself. You can go to some grownups, but if they let you down you can gather some of your friends to help." "I learned that you can't do everything by yourself, you might need a little help." "To have more than one plan." "It takes more than one to do something." "I learned that sometimes people can hurt other people's feelings if they destroy something." "Even though we are just kids we can still make a difference." This last idea—that children can make a positive difference in their world—is at the heart of teaching for social justice in the elementary classroom.

Teaching Against the Grain: Laurie's Fourth Grade

Laurie teaches in an ethnically and economically diverse working-class community in a large city. With 35 students crammed in her classroom, few curricular resources, and no support for social justice teaching among her colleagues, Laurie creates her own literature-based, social justice–oriented units because she believes that "you can work to make the world a better place even if it's your own very little world."

Laurie is mindful of teaching for and about social justice every day, through social studies topics, children's literature, and the problem-solving and decision-making opportunities she extends to her students. While the district's expectations are focused on students' literacy and math development, Laurie finds time to incorporate class meetings for addressing conflicts and community building along with thematic-based lessons (see some of Laurie's class meeting practices in Chapter 2).

Central to all of her work with children is the concept of student voice. Laurie encourages her students to ask questions, to express their views on controversial issues, and even to question authority—which sometimes leads other teachers in the school to say that her students have "too much free will," a comment that leads Laurie to conclude that her efforts are succeeding.

Laurie's classroom extends into the community, as guest speakers come to the school to teach her students and Laurie takes her students on field trips into the city. When the class was studying Helen Keller, Laurie invited speakers from a local school for the deaf and from the Braille Institute. During a unit on immigration, someone from the Chinese Cultural Organization came to her class. As part of their study of African American history, Laurie took her students to the African American Museum. All of these experiences provide opportunities for Laurie's students to ask questions of experts and to learn about multiple perspectives on the topics at hand.

While Laurie asserts that one can teach for social justice in regard to any topic, she generally chooses a broad yearlong theme that allows her to integrate the study of many individuals and grassroots movements aimed at social justice goals. One of the themes she found most inspiring was Freedom Fighters. Students read books about different individuals who fought for freedom, including famous people such as Martin Luther King Jr., Helen Keller, Rosa Parks, and Frederick Douglass, yet Laurie also included "names you don't hear a whole lot," as she wanted her students to learn not just about the remarkable efforts of a few but also about the simple things ordinary people can do to make the world better in small ways.

In part because Laurie's school emphasizes students' literacy development over other subjects, Laurie makes sure to include ample opportunities for reading within her social justice teaching. During the Freedom Fighters theme, Laurie gave her students "tons of books, information, and articles on a variety of different freedom fighters." Students then selected one individual to study in depth and portray in a monologue for the class. Laurie often buys classroom sets of the novels she has chosen (with her own money) and then builds her curriculum around the books. "We read a little piece of the novel every day," Laurie explained, "and we talk about it at great length. We do a number of projects around it: writing projects, art projects, science work, social studies research work, and trips related to those themes. Everything is related to the themes."

Laurie is successful with her teaching, in part, because she is resourceful. She takes advantage of local organizations and speakers as well as free curricular materials from the Southern Poverty Law Center's Teaching Tolerance program. She saves the class sets of books she purchases (usually just one or two sets a year) to create an extensive library that she can continue to use in her teaching.

Laurie is also resourceful in finding support for her social justice teaching. While she does not feel that any of her colleagues in the school are allies in this work, she does find support through a local teacher's cooperative, a local writing group, and progressive national educational organizations that sponsor workshops and seminars she occasionally attends. She is also an avid reader of social justice literature and attends the local Quaker meeting and Quaker conferences (though she does not self-identify as a Quaker) because she appreciates the ways they educate their children.

Laurie prevails in teaching for social justice in some of the most difficult circumstances a teacher could face. Through creativity, perseverance, and resourcefulness, Laurie's experiences in the classroom illustrate that social justice teaching in the elementary school can work for teachers and children, not just in social justice–supportive schools, but in any school where a teacher cares enough to make a difference.

CONCLUSION

Social justice teaching involves taking critical, creative, and sometimes subversive approaches to reinventing the social studies curriculum. While such efforts can be lonely at times, many of us can find support in collaborating with our colleagues or our students' parents. In a few cases, some of us are lucky enough to teach in a school whose culture, mission, and faculty embrace the principles of social justice. And all of us have the opportunity to connect with like-minded educators through a national or regional social justice education organization. Whether we teach in a social justice oriented school or feel like the "Lone Ranger" of social justice, we can reinvent our social studies lessons to be student-centered, collaborative, experiential, and critical. Like Rob, Rebecca, and Laurie, we can give our students opportunities for voice and choice in the classroom, thus facilitating their development as empowered learners and activists.

Reflection Exercises

1. Choose one teacher quote from this chapter that inspires you and be ready to explain to a partner why you chose this quote. What does the quote indicate about your perspective on teaching for social justice?
2. Focus on either Rob's, Laurie's, or Rebecca's teaching vignettes and compare their classroom experiences with the social justice education characteristics in Chapter 1. Which are strengths of their teaching? Which could be developed further?
3. As teachers we can be creative in our attempts to meet district and state standards or we can be resistant. What are the advantages and disadvantages of each approach?

5

Social Justice Themes and Skills

Some of my units are Changes, Civil Rights, Immigration, and Migrant Workers. And at the beginning of each unit I ask the students, "What do you already know about this?" And then I ask them, "Well, what do you want to learn?" And their questions are listed and put in our classroom, and it guides our inquiry and activities. And I also ask them, "What kind of activities do you want to do to learn about these things?" And that really drives the instruction.

—Rebecca, Grade 3 teacher

SOCIAL JUSTICE THEMES

Civil Rights, Immigration, Migrant Workers—these are not the standard fare for social studies units in most third-grade classrooms. According to the expanding environments model, the third-grade year is typically devoted to studying the local community and perhaps comparing the students' community to other similar or different communities in the nation or world.

In the previous chapter, I discussed how one can adapt traditional social studies topics for a social justice–oriented curriculum. While it is not necessary for us to abandon or go beyond the standard social studies curricular themes in order to teach for social justice, our efforts can often be more effective if we teach social justice themes directly. In this chapter I explore themes that are most relevant in teaching elementary social studies for social justice. These themes are divided into three categories: human rights, democracy, and conservation.

Human Rights

Concern for human rights has pervaded societies and cultures throughout history. While some people identify human rights as a recent Western invention associated with the development of documents such as the U.S. Bill of Rights and the United Nations Declaration of Human Rights, in fact human rights can be traced to Native American tribes and ancient Asian cultures, as well as more widely asserted beginnings in ancient Israel and Greece (Berger, 1977).

Most human rights proponents would agree that *human rights* are those conditions, practices, and experiences due every human being by virtue of being human. Human rights include both material support as well as tolerance, respect, and relating to all people with dignity. These aspects of human rights mirror the definition of *social justice* offered in Chapter 2, yet the term *human rights*, perhaps because of its association with U.S. and U.N. documents, is more widely accepted and readily understood and less politicized than the concept of social justice.

Human rights lessons in the elementary social studies curriculum can focus on learning about injustice in our society and world. They should also highlight people and movements that have worked for greater justice for oppressed or marginalized groups of people or the world as a whole. Each has its place in the curriculum. Learning about injustice can awaken young children's empathy and concern for others. And studying effective movements and historical events resulting in greater justice can inspire students, giving them not only hope but also practical strategies to work for social change now and in the future.

The study of U.S. history provides a rich opportunity for teaching about discriminatory and prejudicial acts as well as positive steps for human rights. Powerful examples of injustice can be found in the topics of slavery, colonialism, Chinese railroad workers, child labor, migrant labor, and the Great Depression. Historical grassroots movements for justice include the Underground Railroad; the Civil Rights, women's rights, and children's rights movements; the Peace movement; the Latino movement; and efforts to pass United Nations human rights documents.

In the upper elementary years, we can also include studies of global justice and injustice. For example, learning about the Holocaust, apartheid, the Spanish conquest of the Incas, Columbus's "discovery" of America and the subsequent treatment of Native Americans by European immigrants allow students to explore how unjustly people have often treated those who are different from them. Many of these same examples have led to examples of global justice, such as the ending of apartheid, the trials of war criminals from World War II, and countries across the globe gaining their independence.

Looking at injustice and justice in current events is also important. As teachers, we can focus on helping our students make connections between historical events, present-day circumstances, and opportunities to be history makers as they work on social issues themselves in the school or community. Current social issues that can be studied in the elementary curriculum include: hunger, homelessness, racism, sexism, labor issues, poverty, stereotyping, unemployment, and homophobia. And again, each of these areas provides the opportunity to learn about national or global efforts to solve or lessen these problems.

Paying attention to the news can lead to opportunities to connect current events with students' interests. Jesse, a teacher in rural Colorado, brought in an article and photo about Jimmy Carter winning the Nobel Peace Prize. Jesse noted, "Because Carter was one of the people that tried to get Egypt and Israel to sit down and work out their differences, our Palestinian student could relate to that." Jesse then introduced Martin Luther King Jr., via a recently purchased book, as "another person who won the Nobel Peace Prize." This example also illustrates how we can find opportunities for "teachable moments" that connect current events with history.

One of the simplest approaches to teaching about positive actions for social justice is to study role models who have worked for human rights. As Rob pointed out (see Chapter 4), "The concept of social justice is not easy, social justice movements are not easy. People are." Martin Luther King Jr., Rosa Parks, Harriet Tubman, Sojourner Truth, Frederick Douglass, Ghandi, Mother Theresa, Helen Keller, Ruby Bridges, Jimmy Carter, and the Dalai Lama are just a few of the many human rights activists children can study. Children can also learn about specific types of people who worked for human rights such as African American inventors, Freedom Fighters, and Nobel Peace Prize winners.

As children study people who have worked for human rights, it is important to point out that no individual works completely in isolation. While leaders play an important role, long-term change is most often the result of many people's efforts. Social studies textbooks often tend to emphasize the power of the individual over collective efforts. For example, Rosa Parks is often regarded as single-handedly responsible for starting the Montgomery Bus Boycott, when in fact the African American community had already planned the boycott and was waiting for a prominent person in the community, such as Parks, to be arrested in order to begin the boycott (Kohl, 1994b).

Democracy

Learning about basic democratic principles, how our democratic government works, and how to work for change using the democratic process are important if citizens are to effectively participate in and improve society. One of the best means for learning the principles and importance of democratic governance is through the practice of living democracy in the classroom. Students can only learn to understand and appreciate the democratic ideals of equality, liberty, responsibility, and community by living them. Opportunities for democratic practice in daily classroom life are frequent and include making choices and decisions about curricular as well as extracurricular activities, creating rules, evaluating class activities, and sharing ideas and opinions during class discussions.

In addition to engaging in democratic practice, the elementary social studies curriculum should include content on a variety of topics related to democracy and government: our local, state, and federal government; rules and laws; the U.S. Constitution; government documents such as the Pledge of Allegiance and the Bill of Rights; and both traditional and controversial strategies for civic action (e.g., voting, lobbying, boycotts, strikes, and civil disobedience).

As we teach the notion of what *citizenship* means in a democratic society, we need to be mindful of the many aspects of being an effective citizen. Kahne and Westheimer (1996) assert that there are three types of citizens: "good" (or obedient) citizens, participatory citizens, and justice-oriented citizens. In fact, each of these types is related to specific actions that work together to comprise effective citizenship. *Good* or *obedient citizens* pay their taxes, obey laws, and don't interfere with others' rights to live as they so choose as long as no one is being harmed. *Participatory citizens* get more involved in the civic life of their community, through voting, attending public meetings, and helping out with community service. It is only the *justice-oriented citizen* who seeks to change those aspects of the community that do not support everyone's right to be a productive and participatory member of society.

While all three types of civic behavior play an important role in a functioning democracy, in order to create a socially just society we need to go beyond making contributions to the status quo and question prevailing norms and practices and seek to create meaningful changes in the face of injustice. Teaching students the skills to create change through respectful dialogue and deliberation and creative use of the democratic process is essential. Many of these skills are listed in a section on "Skills for Activism" later in this chapter.

Elementary social studies curricula often require teaching more traditional and admittedly less controversial content in regard to democracy and government. For example, the mandated curriculum materials may focus on learning about central figures in U.S. government (such as George Washington and other U.S. presidents) and the state flag, flower, and song. When teaching these topics, we can encourage students to question what they are learning. For example, when discussing the Pledge of Allegiance, we can teach children what the words mean, or otherwise "deconstruct" the Pledge. In Gaia's class, children spontaneously added, "we wish" to the end of the pledge, in recognition of the fact that our society has not yet achieved liberty and justice for *all*.

Conservation

Conservation (or, in more elementary school–friendly terms, caring for the earth) is the third component of social justice education because we cannot attain social justice as a global society without also considering the environment. This perspective is supported by two assertions. First, animals and plants are important parts of our living world and thus need to be respected, honored, and cared for in their own right. Second, environmental crises are inseparable from social crises. Cultures and ethnic groups who are subjected to discrimination often suffer because of environmental problems in their communities. Examples include U.S. inner cities, in which disproportionate amounts of toxic waste and pollution are literally dumped on those with the least racial and economic power, and cultures in third world countries whose land is used to farm export crops rather than feed the people who live there. Thus, given that various social groups experience ecological problems differently, any analysis of social justice must address the connections between racism, classism, environmentalism, and economic development (Furman & Gruenewald, 2004).

Again, we need to teach about both injustice and justice. Our students can learn from many examples of environmental injustice as well as from stories of action taken by citizens and governments to preserve our natural resources. Each type of injustice has its social change counterpart. For example, when teaching about endangered species, we can introduce students to the animal rights movement and global efforts like the moratorium on whaling. Because some environmental problems can seem intractable and overwhelming, we can put the slogan "Think globally, act locally" into practice with our students. For instance, in a unit on hunger, we can teach our students about the many positive attempts in our community to provide healthy food options for everyone. In my community, this list would include community gardens, the Table-to-Table program (bringing donated food from grocery stores to local soup kitchens and homeless shelters), farmer's markets, and community-supported agriculture through which individuals can purchase shares of local gardens and receive a weekly box of produce.

Conservation can also be taught in concert with geography studies. What are the unique features of various environments and landforms? How do humans abuse and/or care for these environments? Studies of the pollution of our air, water, and land can be accompanied by hands-on projects to set up a schoolwide recycling program, clean up an area near a local river, or advocate for no-smoking restaurants in the community.

It is also illuminating when examining the use of natural resources across the globe to ask students to research and chart their own consumption of food, energy, water, and so forth. What they will quickly learn is that most U.S. citizens use three to four times their share of the earth's resources. Ensuing discussion on this troublesome social justice issue can lead to further efforts to make personal lifestyle changes or to work for environmental changes in the school or community. Students can also get involved with national and international efforts to improve the well-being of the planet. One promising effort in this regard is the Carbon Neutral program, which asks individuals and businesses to plant trees in order to counteract the greenhouse gas emissions produced by personal travel and resource consumption (see http://www.carbonneutral.com).

SOCIAL JUSTICE SKILLS

A social justice–oriented social studies curriculum goes beyond concepts and facts associated with themes related to human rights, democracy, and conservation. An essential aspect of this curriculum for the elementary school also includes teaching children a variety of skills for both making sense of and making a difference in the world. Facilitating students' skill development is important so that they can lead productive lives themselves as well as work for social justice in their communities. "A social justice classroom equips children not only to change the world but also to maneuver in the one that exists" (Bigelow et al., 1994, p. 5). This dual focus may feel like walking a tightrope at times, yet we must prepare our students for both the present world they encounter on a daily basis and the future world we are hoping will be the result of our collective social change efforts.

Social justice education places considerable emphasis on co-construction of knowledge and "big ideas," yet this focus should not be taken to imply that there is little attention to skill development. Using prior skills to learn new ones is an essential part of the work (Cochran-Smith, 2004), and before students can effect change in existing school or community situations, they must first develop skills in how to learn about, analyze, and ask questions about the world. Thus very young students may be spending more time on basic academic skill development (e.g., reading and writing) while upper elementary students will spend a greater portion of time on using their reading and writing skills for social change. We can divide skills for a social justice–oriented social studies program into two broad categories: skills for "reading the world" and skills for activism.

Skills for Reading the World

Many skills are important in our efforts to help our students critically read the world around them. Some of these are basic reading and language arts skills (reading, writing, listening, speaking, and other communication skills). Others could best be classified as critical thinking skills (comparing and contrasting, problem solving, categorizing, questioning, analyzing, predicting, empathizing, making connections, recognizing common ground, finding relevance, assessing one's learning). Molly teaches these skills as the need arises. "It doesn't necessarily have to be a separate unit on each of these things," she noted. "It could be one lesson on many of these things and as you continue the project, they keep developing these skills. So you're not teaching them as discrete skills, because it's project-oriented and child-centered."

Molly bases her instruction on a well-known fact about powerful teaching and learning. Students will have more interest in learning a skill, learn it more thoroughly, and have more likelihood of retaining their use of the skill if they are given an opportunity to use the skill in a meaningful and authentic way in relation to a project or activity to which they are invested. The familiar adage "Use it or lose it" is relevant here as well. Students need more than one opportunity to use a skill if they are to see its relevance and retain the skill over time.

Another aspect of reading the world is evaluating the source for any given information or facts. Bringing a variety of resources into the classroom not only gives students multiple perspectives on a topic, but analyzing and comparing different sources of information can also help children learn to detect bias and check for accuracy. Students can develop "critical literacy" skills as they analyze current events, primary sources, and historians' accounts of the past. Key questions we can ask when guiding students in their analysis include the following: What is the source of this information? What perspective on the issue or event is being promoted? Are there other sources of information that offer different perspectives? Whose story is being told and who is being left out? All of these questions will help students realize that we all have perspectives that are informed by our experiences, our values, and our prior learning. What is essential is to attempt to identify our own and others' perspectives, not in an effort to locate the "truth," but to gain greater insight into the different opinions and attempt to develop an evidence-based understanding of the issue under study.

Skills for Activism

The second set of skills essential in a social justice oriented social studies curriculum are those needed for community activism. These include skills to gather information and data (e.g., interviewing, note taking, identifying and consulting experts, talking to adults, reading social cues and body language, talking on the phone, using e-mail and the Internet) and strategies for organizing the information collected (e.g., cooperating, working in a group, making graphs, analyzing statistics, citing sources). Strategies for conveying information to others (e.g., writing a persuasive letter, making a protest sign, giving a speech, debating, making a presentation, creating a Web site, writing a public service announcement) and specific activism strategies (e.g., fund-raising, organizing drives and campaigns, and circulating a petition) are also useful. Many activism skills are context specific. For example, one teacher taught her students to create a museum exhibition and to serve as tour guides. Again, all of the skills for activism will be learned more effectively if students use them more than once in authentic situations of concern to them.

Molly identified an additional skill for activism, which is especially applicable for group activities or service projects involving people who speak different languages. "One of the skills I teach my kids is looking for cognates, using context to try to understand what someone is saying when they're not speaking your native language." Molly emphasized the importance of this skill for two reasons: "to empathize with the English language learners and to not be as uptight as monolingual grown-ups are when they hear someone speaking another language." Thus the skill is more than understanding what someone is saying, it is also about developing empathy and being comfortable and accepting in situations where different languages are spoken.

While skills and topics have been discussed separately in this chapter, in reality we do not usually separate process from content in the elementary classroom. Students can be learning content about a variety of social justice topics while also learning skills to read the world and practicing activism skills in their school and community. In the next section I describe an example of a social justice unit on a frequently taught human rights topic, the Civil Rights Movement, illustrating how content, skills, and teaching strategies can be integrated to facilitate effective learning for children.

A SAMPLE UNIT: THE CIVIL RIGHTS MOVEMENT

Kara teaches a unit on the Civil Rights Movement to her combined second- and third-grade class during the winter months each year. First, she breaks the class into groups to do a web about what they know about Martin Luther King Jr. and the Civil Rights Movement. Often they know very little; the few facts they list are usually associated with the assassination of Martin Luther King Jr. Following the small-group web construction, Kara facilitates a class discussion in which each student shares a point from the group web.

Then, with a partner, students choose a book to read from the many Kara has collected on the Civil Rights Movement. Two of her favorites are *I Am Rosa Parks* (Parks & Haskins, 1999), an easy reader on Rosa Parks, and *Cracking the Wall: The Struggles of the Little Rock Nine* (Lucas, 1997). After they have read a book, they write down things that they learned on Post-it notes and add them to the appropriate spot on their web. Each student then shares something that they learned through their reading with the whole class.

Kara integrates her social studies unit with both reading and math. During their reading-group time, students read books on various aspects of the Civil Rights Movement. Kara has collected multiple copies of several books at different reading levels for this purpose. The students discuss and answer comprehension questions about what they are reading. Kara also reads aloud from various books to the whole class during story time. In math, Kara constructs word problems using dates and numbers in the Movement.

After this introduction to the unit, Kara moves the focus of her lessons beyond Martin Luther King Jr. to others who made a difference in the Civil Rights Movement. "This year," explained Kara, "we focused on Rosa Parks for a week, then the next week we focused on the kids who integrated schools (Ruby Bridges and The Little Rock Nine), then on to Sheyann Webb and the Voting Rights Movement." Sheyann and her friend Rachel West, at eight years old (the same age as many of Kara's students), were the youngest participants in the march from Selma to Montgomery, Alabama, known as Bloody Sunday.

Kara employs many active strategies in her teaching. Students construct and act out role-plays and skits based on the events they are studying. Also, Kara teaches her class at least one freedom song each week of the unit.

Critical thinking is an important element of Kara's teaching. As students watch videos (Southern Poverty Law Center's Teaching Tolerance program has several that Kara finds useful) and news clips on events from the Movement, Kara teaches them how to discern real footage, past and present, from simulated clips. The students also learn how to critically evaluate historical evidence and varying perspectives on this time period. For example, Kara gives her students several different accounts of why Rosa Parks refused to give up her seat on the bus and asks students to analyze and evaluate the evidence to decide what they think.

Kara assists her students with exploring cause and effect and the sequencing of events with a time-line activity. Each student chooses a book to read about the Civil Rights Movement. Then they write one important date and event on a Post-it note. Next, they each put their Post-it note on the board in order, making sure that no one else has chosen their event. They then write the date and event on a piece of drawing paper and illustrate the event. Finally, the students construct a "human time line" by having one student at a time come up and stand in a chronologically accurate line, showing their drawing and explaining the event.

While the students learn that the Civil Rights Movement happened many years ago, Kara is careful to emphasize that Martin Luther King Jr. and others who contributed their efforts to the Civil Rights Movement did not rid society of racism; it still exists today. Class discussions help students make personal connections to their experiences of racism and discrimination.

Another essential message in Kara's unit is that "Leaders are important, but one person cannot create a movement." Throughout the unit, students learn that many people were involved, including children. This teaching leads to another important point, that social action can occur in many ways and has relevance to students' everyday lives. Kara supports her students in identifying issues of concern to them and taking appropriate action. For example, Kara's students wrote a letter to the school principal objecting to the cancelation of soccer on the playground. Also many of her students wrote letters to or appeared in front of the school board in an effort to convince them to allow animals back in the classroom.

Kara's unit on the Civil Rights Movement is just one example of effective social justice teaching in the elementary classroom. Chapter 6 on in-class social justice teaching strategies and Chapter 7 on activism and other types of community connections provide many more examples of teaching for and about social justice.

CONCLUSION

While we can teach about social justice topics both within and outside of the standard expanding environments curriculum, teaching themes related to human rights, democracy, and conservation will contribute to the effectiveness of our social justice teaching. Students need to learn about both unjust situations as well as powerful stories of individuals and collective groups who have created positive change in the world. Teaching skills for "reading the world" and engaging in activism are important in the social justice curriculum. In daily classroom life, we can effectively integrate process and content to facilitate students' learning in the classroom and their efforts to make meaningful changes in their school and community.

Reflection Exercises

1. Choose a standard topic from the expanding environments social studies curriculum (K—self, 1—families, 2—neighborhood, 3—community, and so forth). Develop a plan for how you could teach this topic at a suitable grade level from a social justice perspective.
2. Develop a lesson on one of the human rights issues mentioned in this chapter. Choose a grade level and objectives, as well as activities and assessment strategies.
3. Examine Kara's unit on the Civil Rights Movement in relation to the essential characteristics of social justice teaching in Chapter 1. Which are strengths of Kara's teaching? Are there any that she does not address in her unit? What ideas do you have for additions or changes to the unit?

6

Essential Teaching Strategies

I think that to arrive at any conclusion about things being done in an unjust way, you have to ask the right questions. Information in general, but also the way that we teach information in the schools, is very much based on preventing those questions from being asked.
—Colleen, Grades 4–6 language arts resource teacher

Teaching for and about social justice, like all effective teaching, involves using a variety of active learning strategies in the classroom. As Colleen suggests in the quote above, asking the right kinds of questions, ones that make students think critically and creatively rather than just repeating learned facts, is essential. Children's literature, expressive arts, role-play, simulation, and primary sources are also prominent in social justice teaching. What distinguishes our use of these strategies from "just good teaching" (Ladson-Billings, 1992) is their emphasis on empathy, critical thinking, multiple perspectives, and activism. Whether they are part of the planned curriculum or a spontaneous "teachable moment," the ways in which we use a variety of teaching methods empower our students to be critical thinkers and social activists, now and in the future.

This chapter describes how we can use in-class teaching strategies to accomplish social justice education goals. Chapter 7 will address teaching strategies that focus specifically on activism and community connections within and outside of the school. The focus here is on strategies aimed at developing empathy, fostering multiple perspectives, and getting students to ask questions and develop their own opinions about issues that matter. The specific strategies explored in this chapter include thematic teaching, children's literature, questions, role-play and simulations, primary sources, and visual and performing arts.

THEMATIC APPROACH

Using a thematic approach can be an effective means for meeting our social justice teaching goals by maximizing the amount of time spent on social justice content and skills in the school day. This approach involves placing social studies at the center of the curriculum and teaching reading, writing, art, and occasionally science and math using the social studies thematic content. Often a theme is broad and carried out over the entire school year. For example, a yearlong study on water could incorporate both science and social studies content. The social studies aspects of the curriculum would focus on how people across time and place use, misuse, and care for water as a natural resource. Teaching one social studies theme for the school year allows us to go into great depth, rather than just skimming the surface of many topics.

If time during the school day does not allow for in-depth teaching of all required subjects, we can still study themes comprehensively through a process of rotation. Risa, a first-grade teacher in Chicago, alternates teaching thematic social studies and science units throughout the school year.

> I think that it's more cohesive to the students and clearer if we're just focusing on one major topic at a time. And exploring that topic in depth makes kids really feel like they're experts and really feel knowledgeable about that topic and be able to sort of think critically about it. You can only really start to think critically about something if you have a pretty solid foundation of knowledge about it.

Risa's points are well taken. If we expect students to critically analyze a topic, evaluate multiple perspectives presented in a variety of resources, and engage as activists with what they have learned, we cannot just have them complete a 2- to 4-week unit based largely on a brief treatment of the topic in their social studies textbook.

Teaching social studies thematically provides the opportunity to teach students basic literacy skills within a meaningful social justice context. Laurie teaches an integrated curriculum where everything except for math is based on a yearlong theme that includes seven novels read by all of her fourth graders. "Explorers, Discoverers, and Pioneers"

past, but also reflect on similar circumstances for themselves or others in the present. *Sam and the Times of Trouble* by F. P. Heide is a historical fiction book about the war in Lebanon. Kara found this book effective "for just having the kids think and wonder and ask questions and empathize with kids who might be living through a war, even if it wasn't the present one in Iraq." Thus historical fiction can help students feel linked with children in history and make connections between the past and the present.

Children's literature can also serve as a catalyst for students taking action. Lindsey begins her "Making a Difference" unit by reading many stories about creative and heroic young people. Her students find examples of activism and become inspired to read more books, go online to do further research, and then develop their own projects to "make a difference." Some types of activism can even involve books. For example, some of Lindsey's students became reading partners with struggling readers in a primary classroom down the hall. Other literacy-based service experiences involve making books for babies or preschoolers and reading to senior citizens.

All of these examples of teaching practice make clear that using children's literature to teach about and for social justice goes far beyond just taking a book off the shelf for the traditional after-lunch story time to settle children down before afternoon academics. Ensuing discussions on the reading are an important part of students' learning from the reading. In addition to silent reading or listening to a read-aloud, students can also partner with younger students to read books and engage in related activities. Bruce's third graders worked with first graders to read books about stereotypes and then complete a questionnaire identifying both the stereotypes and how people "busted" them. Bruce summed up some of the many reasons why using children's literature to teach for social justice is so effective. "I go through literature because kids love it and it's more accessible for them than if you just talk about it as an abstract idea. I think it's a resource that's accessible to you too so you don't have to always invent something—it's right there."

QUESTIONS

Critical thinking is an essential element of social justice education, and critical analysis of a book, an opinion, or a historical event begins with asking questions. Questions initiate activism as well. Applying a critical, questioning perspective to their lives, students can explore the reasons for present conditions and design strategies for changing them (Nieto, 1999).

One of the ways we can best encourage a questioning attitude on the part of our students, is to ask them questions that do not have one right answer, questions that require them to engage deeply with ideas and to consider their own views and values. As some students are more verbal than others and some need time to process their ideas, it is helpful to use both talking and writing as strategies for answering questions. For example, Millicent tries to "invoke a lot of emotion" in her students through discussion and journaling. She asks them questions such as the following: What would you do if . . . ? What would you feel if . . . ? What if this happened, how would you feel? Journaling and discussion can be combined effectively by asking students to first write then to participate in a class discussion, sharing what they wish to from their journals.

When asking students challenging questions, it is important to give them enough background knowledge, informed by a variety of perspectives and sources, to develop a reasoned point of view. Kris believes in challenging her second graders to question what they hear and what's in books. "You should always be questioning things," she tells her students, "not just accepting them for what people tell you, but always kind of delve in a little deeper."

Local newspapers are an excellent resource for looking at multiple perspectives, as articles will frequently include both sides of an issue. Often the author of the article and people quoted within it are available to come to school and talk with students about their perspectives. It is very helpful to have students generate questions ahead of time to ask community members who come to the classroom. This exercise in and of itself promotes critical thinking and learning about civic participation. Encourage students to ask open-ended, respectful questions that address their concerns and the opinions of those whom they are interviewing.

How do we initiate students' interest in appropriate and relevant news articles? As teachers, we can read the newspaper ourselves and bring in interesting articles or we can order a classroom set of papers to be delivered to the school once a week. Either way, children's interests should guide the choice of local issues or events to discuss and explore further. For example, Jesse's second and third graders focused on an article about prairie dogs who were digging up the school grounds and creating a safety hazard. Their central question, put to both guest speakers and themselves, was: Should the prairie dogs be annihilated or saved? This is an example of a current event that has a direct connection to children's lives, but we can also choose articles that relate to topics in our social studies curriculum.

When listening to students' opinions, there is a balance to be maintained between respecting their right to have their own views and ideas and, at the same time, challenging them to explain their views and to provide evidence for their opinions. Kara put it this way: "I don't believe in just telling thcm what I think they should believe. I believe more in dialogue, and I've found that with every class I've had that there's been very wide viewpoints on a topic." As students dialogue, they can build upon and challenge each other's ideas, further refining and testing their ideas about an issue as they engage not only with each other but with guest speakers, Internet sources, print resources, and their own experiences in the school and community.

ROLE-PLAY AND SIMULATIONS

Role-plays and simulations help elementary students understand and relate to people and events from another time or place. Playacting is a natural fit for children, as many engage in it during their free time. Gaia assists her kindergartners in "trying to get inside somebody else's skin, get a little empathy going" through role-plays based on biographies she reads aloud on Helen Keller, Louis Braille, Harriet Tubman, and Frederick Douglass. Role-plays related to *ableism*—prejudices against individuals with disabilities (e.g., being blind or diabetic)—can be used to increase students' awareness and empathy and decrease their fear. Effective role-play encourages students to step outside of their own shoes and see things from someone else's perspective.

Role-play involves students choosing a person from the present or past, often a famous person, and either giving a monologue or acting in a skit pretending to be that person. For instance, when one of Laurie's students brought in loads of information on Frederick Douglass during their study of Civil Rights Movements in America, Laurie had every student research and then role-play one of the Freedom Fighters. Students thus had the opportunity to learn in-depth about the person they role-played but also to learn about many others from their peers' presentations.

A simulation, as used in social studies education, is usually an imaginary replication of a historical event. Often a simulation involves students playing the roles of specific people. For example, Kris's second graders did a simulation about Rosa Parks and the Montgomery Bus Boycott. Key roles were Rosa, the bus driver, and the police officer. Many of the students played the "ordinary people" who made the boycott successful. Kris noted how powerful the simulation experience was, especially for one student. "This one little girl just became Rosa Parks, like that's who she was. She just had this sense of being a strong woman and standing up for what was right. [In her writing] she talked about how she felt like she was Rosa Parks and really standing up for something that needed to be changed."

Through role-plays and simulations, teachers are meeting both social justice and academic content objectives. Students can discover the personal motivation and life experiences that contribute to someone like Frederick Douglass or Rosa Parks becoming an activist while also learning about significant historical events in U.S. history. While commercial simulations for elementary social studies are readily available, upper elementary students can also write their own simulations by first writing the story of an event and then deciding on the roles. Students can write a script or, for an easier format, ad-lib their parts.

PRIMARY SOURCES

Like role-play, primary sources are a means for connecting students with history in concrete and meaningful ways. Primary sources are materials directly from a time period (e.g., journals, diaries, newspaper articles, songs, government documents, letters, public notices, transcripts of speeches, photos, and so forth). In contrast with textbook excerpts or historian's accounts, primary sources allow students to analyze and interpret historical evidence and to construct their own understandings of historical events. For example, Sue used slave journals and Sojourner Truth's speech "Ain't I a Woman" to help her students understand the past and become inspired to engage in community activism.

Photos are an especially effective primary source for the elementary classroom as they can be used at any grade level regardless of students' reading abilities. They can also be very effective in facilitating students' understanding of and empathy for others. Kara used photos to help her second- and third-grade ESL students look at war from a perspective not often included in the U.S. media:

> We had a few [photos] at that time from our local newspaper and U.S. sources. The rest were all international sources. We had maybe 30 photos that we thought from one way or another showed the Iraqis' point of view. The kids each chose one that spoke to them and wrote about it. And I felt that really did a switch in the kid's mind of being able to see that there was another side to this, that there wasn't just the United States' side and *our* soldiers' side.

Students generally enjoy working with primary sources because they present history as a mystery or a puzzle to be solved using the available evidence. Working with primary sources also gives students a strong message about multiple perspectives. There is no one correct version of the past; people's views of historical events are very different depending on their values, beliefs, and experiences. For example, Paul Revere would likely tell us a very different story than a British soldier about the events leading up to and the significance of "the midnight ride."

One way to illustrate how primary sources can lead to different understandings of history is to divide the class into small groups and give each group a different primary source on the same event or topic from a time period. Ask students to share their understanding of the event based on the primary source they analyzed. They will quickly realize that one's understanding is greatly influenced by the sources of information available. To develop a more thorough understanding of the event, ask students to form new groups that include one person from each of the original groups. Students can then discuss all the sources, and if needed, engage in further research to address any conflicting information.

Primary sources also provide a window into history that students would not have access to otherwise. Reading personal letters and journals written by people in the past emphasizes our common humanity and can help students realize that people across time and place share many similarities, despite their differences. This realization can lead students to feel more empathy and caring for those who are different from themselves, which will hopefully lead to their desire to work for others' rights and well-being.

VISUAL AND PERFORMING ARTS

Another essential strategy for social justice teaching is artistic expression through both visual and performing arts. Student voice is a central component of social justice education and the arts provide additional opportunities for self-expression. From puppetry, dance, and singing to drawing, printmaking, painting, and other visual media, the arts present students with additional ways to express their opinions and values on social justice issues.

Using caption drawings with primary age students can help us assess what young children are learning from their social justice education. This strategy involves the teacher writing a dictated caption under the student's illustration. First, one asks the students what is going on in their pictures and then records the child's thinking at the bottom of the page. This strategy can serve as a check on students' understanding of abstract or unfamiliar concepts. When Molly's students were studying the Underground Railroad, she learned that a few students didn't understand it in the historic sense because they drew pictures of trains under the ground. This example shows how the caption-drawing strategy can expose students' misconceptions of the past.

Music can also be an important component in social justice teaching. Music has played a central role in many human rights movements, from slavery to the Civil Rights Movement to contemporary peace movements. Students can learn to sing songs from the past or write songs to affirm others or to create awareness of injustice. From protest songs to Schoolhouse Rock, there are many opportunities for integrating music in a social justice–oriented social studies curriculum.

Teachers sometimes create songs too. The week I observed in Molly's classroom, the whole school was studying the Constitution, due to a recent federal mandate. Molly and one of the first-grade teachers met over a break to try to figure out a way to teach the Constitution in a meaningful way to primary age children. They came up with a simplified version of the rights in the Bill of Rights and the next day gathered both classes together to sing a song they created (to the tune of "The Twelve Days of Christmas"). "The first right we have is the right to free speech, and freedom and peace for all," sang the students. Thus music and art in the social justice classroom provide opportunities for creativity and expression on the part of both teachers and students.

AND MORE . . .

The strategies discussed in this chapter are just a few of many that could be used to positive effect in a social justice–oriented social studies curriculum. Most of us use maps, charts, videos, computers, and other tools in our daily teaching. Certainly, public speaking, conflict resolution, and cooperative learning could play an important role in social justice education. And while I have not discussed reading, writing, and class discussion generally, these standard activities are an important part of all elementary school teaching. Consider the following creative uses of writing in social justice teaching. In her unit on Native Americans, Jane has her students write letters from different people's points of view, including different tribes and those traveling on wagon trains. Rob incorporates dialogue poems into his U.S. history teaching (see the Teaching Idea at the end of this chapter for a lesson on this strategy). Both Jane's letter writing and Rob's dialogue poems encourage not only writing skills but also empathy for others and exploration of multiple perspectives.

The strategies discussed in this chapter, while not an exhaustive list, are those that are of central importance in a social justice–oriented curriculum because of their consistency with the characteristics of effective social justice education outlined in Chapter 1. I have not mentioned social studies textbooks as important tools for social justice teaching, nor have I highlighted other typical social studies teaching strategies such as reviewing vocabulary lists, coloring maps, taking quizzes, or answering textbook chapter questions. While these activities may take place on occasion, they are not the defining features of a social justice–oriented social studies curriculum. Instead, social justice teaching primarily involves active teaching strategies that contribute to both academic development and social justice education goals.

CONCLUSION

The in-class strategies used by social justice teachers in elementary schools involve their students in thinking critically and creatively about contemporary and historical events. Many of the strategies engage students in considering multiple perspectives and developing empathy for those who live in different times, places, or cultures. Social justice teachers recognize that it is important to engage students' hearts as well as their minds in the learning process and to give them opportunities to express their thoughts and feelings through role-play, simulations, artwork, and singing. Through thematic and literature-based instruction, social justice educators provide students with in-depth, challenging, and meaningful learning experiences in their elementary classrooms.

Teaching Ideas

Children's Literature

1. Choose a unit from your social studies curriculum that is social justice related. Possibilities might include civil rights, human rights, women's rights, all kinds of families, building peaceful communities, or immigration.
2. Locate two children's literature books for the unit you chose.
3. Develop a plan for how you could use one of these books with your class. Will you read it aloud? Purchase a class set? Obtain 5 or 6 copies for a literature circle?
4. Plan your introduction of the book to the class. Consider discussing who the author is and what bias or perspective he or she might have toward the subject of the book. Based on the title, the cover, and perhaps a few sentences at the beginning of the book, ask students, "What do you think this book will be about? Can you guess what the author's message might be?"
5. As you read the book (or as students read the book), plan questions to discuss periodically or to have students respond to in writing. Questions might include asking students about (a) their opinions or personal experiences related to the book, (b) the characters' motivations, thoughts, and feelings, and/or (c) ideas for activism in the school or community.
6. If the book concerns a historical time period or event, encourage students to compare the book with primary source materials or historian's accounts.

What in the book appears to be fact and what is a fiction added by the author?

7. After finishing the book, ask students to consider the author's message. What does the author want you to think and feel as a result of reading this book? Is the author trying to inspire you to do something?

8. Finally, consider possible school-based or community-based service-learning or social action activities related to the book. If students are inspired, coordinate their efforts to make a difference and encourage them to take action on their own time outside of school as well.

Dialogue Poems (For Grades 3–6)

1. Dialogue poems—poems that have two voices or parts that are juxtaposed—are "effective to use where controversy or different opinions might arise" (Bigelow, et al., 1994). The poems can also point out similarities between two people who might not seem to have much in common. These poems can be an especially powerful strategy to get students to appreciate multiple perspectives and empathize with those who have different life experiences. Read the following dialogue poem, representing the voices of an American middle-class teenager and a teenage worker in Pakistan, to the class (Wade, 2004). Choose two readers, A and B. Both students read the line labeled "A & B" together. Then one student reads the line labeled A, followed by the other student reading the line labeled B. Repeat this pattern throughout the poem. After reading the poem, ask students to reflect on and discuss the following questions: What do these two teenagers have in common? How are their lives different? What ideas for social action does this poem inspire?

> *A & B*: I am a teenager.
> *A*: I go to school all day.
> *B*: I work all day.
>
> *A & B*: I wish I could spend more time with my friends.
> *A*: Between sports and homework, I barely have time for video games.
> *B*: I get up before the sun rises and work until after dark.
>
> *A & B*: I keep getting injured.
> *A*: I twisted my knee in soccer the other day.

B: My hands are bloody and sore from sewing soccer balls all day.

A & B: I got in trouble today.
A: Coach was so mad he made me run five extra laps.
B: Boss was so mad he beat me and took away my dinner.

A & B: It's tough being a teenager.
A: I have to feed the dog and take out the garbage.
B: Scavenging through garbage is the only way I can get enough to eat.

A & B: But I have hope for the future.
A: Someday I plan to make enough money to buy a sports car.
B: Someday I hope to go to school and learn what is valuable in life.

2. Put students in pairs (or ask them to find a partner) to create their own dialogue poems. For younger students, omit the line in common and just alternate each voice. Students could choose historical characters (a slave owner and a slave, a Tory and a Revolutionary, a suffragette and a woman who does not believe that women should vote) or contemporary people, famous or ordinary (leaders of different countries, children from different cultures, people from different socioeconomic classes).
3. Invite students to read their poems aloud and to ask each other questions about the poems. Conclude each sharing with having listeners say something they liked or appreciated about the poem.
4. For other dialogue poems and teaching ideas, see Bigelow et al., 1994, and Fleischman, 1988.
5. Use dialogue poems as a springboard to generating ideas for social action. Consider having students write advocacy letters, do fund-raising for an organization, or engage in direct work in the community.

7

Activism and Community Connections

Last year I had a kid who was a really reluctant writer. He never wanted to write more than two sentences although he's a very bright kid; he just hated writing. When we were doing our child labor unit and the kids decided to write to the newspaper and different companies, he was so motivated to get those letters out. I think it was because it was writing for a purpose that he thought was important. It made a big difference for him in his attitude and also in his accomplishments in writing. I think that kids feel that it's real work, it's not just fake work.

—Kara, Grades 2–3 teacher

Social justice education places special emphasis on bridging the gap between the classroom and the community. When students are engaged in meaningful activities with others outside of the classroom, they develop enthusiasm for learning and the community also benefits. Rather than practicing reading and writing or other "fake work," students become immersed in real-world problem solving and applying skills and knowledge learned in the classroom to civic actions. "Education works best when it is grounded, when it merges the skills and knowledge of the community with the skills and knowledge of educators" (Kohl, 1994a, p. 62). Teaching for social justice simply cannot stop at the classroom door. Our efforts to create significant improvements in teaching and learning *within* schools are strengthened by forming strong, interactive connections with communities *beyond* them.

Connecting students with the world beyond the walls of the classroom is essential if students are to experience firsthand opportunities to work for social change. It is through firsthand experience that students can best gain an understanding of social justice issues and the possibilities for addressing them. "I think bringing the world into the classroom is just really critical," states Kris, a Philadelphia-based second-grade teacher. "You know, you can't see school as a separate entity. You really have to look around you and see what's happening." Preparation for community experience begins in the classroom with skill development and planning for venturing out into the community. Learning continues outside of the classroom as students seek out valuable sources of information, collect data, and describe what they have learned.

Thus social justice education is as much about learning *from* the community as it is engaging in social action *for* the community. William Ayers (2004), noted social justice teacher educator, agrees: "Education at its best, then, is linked to freedom, to the ability to see but also to alter, to understand but also to reinvent, to know and also to transform the world" (p. 21).

Teachers use many strategies for connecting students with the world outside the classroom walls. Sometimes students don't have to go farther than the playground or the other classrooms in the school to find injustices they want to change. Teachers bring the local community into the classroom via guest speakers and indirect service activities. Students also venture out into the community to participate in hands-on service-learning projects, take a field trip, or attend a community rally.

All of these strategies contribute to opportunities for students to engage in concrete learning and real-world problem solving. Classroom-community connections teach students that social change is more successful when we work together, drawing on the strengths of the entire community. And when students engage in accomplishing a real task that is respected in the world beyond school, they are more likely to understand why they need to acquire basic skills and then work harder to learn them (Fried, 2001). Community connections and activism provide rich opportunities for social justice work.

COMMUNITY CONNECTIONS

We can build meaningful connections between our students and the community by bringing community members into the classroom and taking our students out into the community. The two primary strategies discussed here, guest speakers and field trips, illustrate the power of these experiences for social justice teaching.

Guest Speakers

Bringing the community into the classroom through guest speakers is an effective means for promoting multiple perspectives or different cultural views on an issue. Guest speakers can include local community activists, artists, people from different cultures, people with disabilities, experts on community issues, local politicians, and elderly individuals who can shed light on past events that the class is studying.

Jeffrey, a fifth- and sixth-grade teacher in a rural Colorado town, assists students in being successful community advocates with input from a variety of guest speakers. When a local recreation center was about to be bumped out of the way by a golf course project, Jeffrey brought in city councillors and people from the recreation field to talk about recreation centers and golf courses. After the students learned about the different perspectives, they wrote letters to the local paper advocating for the recreation center. Jeffrey noted, "I think we were helpful in getting the rec center built first. The golf course came along afterwards." Jeffrey's class's efforts provide an example of how teachers can link guest speakers with writing advocacy letters.

A guest speaker can share about events from a personal standpoint that is powerful and fosters students' empathy. The elementary years are an important time period for developing empathy, the ability to understand another's sadness, joy, or anger. Empathy skills developed early on lay the foundation for a concern for social justice in later years. Hopefully, children who can empathize with others will become adults who have compassion for people who are poor, marginalized, discriminated against, or oppressed. Thus introducing elementary-age students to various perspectives and life experiences through guest speakers can be a key step in the process of creating social justice advocates.

Guest speakers can give students a window into another time and place or help them question their views when they might not otherwise. Kara shared, "We had a guest speaker who was a veteran of the war in Vietnam and he came during a war unit and talked about what it was like to be a young idealistic soldier and to go in and really experience what war was like—that was very powerful." When students talk to an older African American activist who was jailed during the Civil Rights Movement or an Iowa farmer who tried to make ends meet during the Great Depression, students develop a very different understanding of history than they would by reading the few sentences devoted to these historical events in their social studies textbooks.

Parents are readily available to be effective guest speakers in the classroom. Pearl, an African American first-grade teacher, brings in parents to counter cultural stereotypes. "I have them come in so the students are also learning about different parents and the jobs that they do, and they're not just stereotyping." She is especially concerned with the image of African American males. She asks black male police officers to come in dressed in plain clothes rather than their uniforms. "And then they ask the children, 'Who do you think I am and what do you think I do?'" One of the best ways to counter stereotypes is to have students directly interact with people who do not fit the typecast.

Guiding students to ask good questions is an important aspect of maximizing their opportunity to learn from community speakers. A good strategy is to have students generate questions beforehand that are relevant to them and then send the questions ahead of time to the guest speaker. Prepared speakers can more effectively address students' concerns and thus engage greater interest from their audience. And since questions are an important aspect of social justice education, teaching several lessons on how to ask respectful and interesting questions will aide students in other aspects of their social justice education as well.

Field Trips

Another type of experience to connect students and the local community is a field trip that highlights social justice issues and engages students in critical analysis. June, an early career teacher in Oakland, California, takes her third graders to Angel Island, an immigration station for Chinese people coming to the West Coast. She noted both the difficulty and the power of her experience. June finds it hard "to present this stuff without it being a downer or scary or hard for them to kind of digest. Because you can't give the whole history of it, it's too complex." However, she also notes that for some students at least, the field trip is a very moving experience:

> They see that sometimes people were stuck on that Island for up to 2 years, waiting to get allowed into the United States. In the men's barracks, people were etching poems in the walls being so

frustrated and sad that they were there. In a book, they have the Chinese characters of the poems that were scratched into the walls. Some of the kids in my class read Chinese so it can really resonate with them.

Powerful experiences such as this enable students to gain a deeper empathy for those in the past as well as consider the present-day connections and opportunities for action. In the case of Angel Island, students could look at how prejudice and discrimination toward the Chinese and other cultures still exist today and then develop a plan for creating greater equal opportunity or stronger cross-cultural interactions and appreciation.

Field trips must be accompanied by reflection and discussion if they are to fulfill their potential as social justice learning experiences. We need to encourage our students to examine the perspectives on social justice issues promoted by the agency, historical site, or other location visited. We must also think carefully about where to take our students on field trips and make sure that they will encounter artifacts and information that will teach them about the legacy of justice and injustice in our society.

ACTIVISM

There are many opportunities for students to engage in social action on issues of interest to them. Some of the options—such as letter writing, indirect service projects, and school-based activism—can be carried out without leaving the school grounds. Other strategies involve taking students out into the local community to engage in direct service or participate in community rallies and marches.

Writing Letters

Letter writing can be a powerful advocacy strategy. Students might write to the principal about a school-based problem or to the mayor about a concern they have in their community. They can write to their city councillors, the governor, or even the president of the United States. Students could also write pen pal letters to children in South Africa, Iraq, or Israel. These are just a few of the possibilities for how letter writing can help students learn about their world, express their views, and work for social change. Because of the power of purposeful writing, ideally every major writing assignment should have a real audience outside the school.

Sometimes letter writing leads to other types of social action as well. When Sue's third graders wrote to California Governor Davis about the unfair distribution of resources in their state's schools and communities, one of her students had the opportunity to read her letter aloud at a press conference.

Letter writing on controversial issues must be structured carefully to be effective. Pam's third and fourth graders became concerned about vivisection at the local university and wrote letters to the university professors protesting their use of live animals for scientific learning. Pam didn't read all the letters before mailing them and some of the children had written inflammatory and disrespectful statements. The researchers were upset and let Pam know. But because Pam welcomed diverse perspectives in her classroom and was open to her students' learning from the community, they had an engaging dialogue with the scientists and also visited and observed the animals at a nearby medical research lab.

Pam's experience highlights several important aspects of letter-writing experiences. First, we must teach students how to write respectful letters, even when they are voicing concern or dissent. Second, as teachers, we are responsible for the content of students' letters and should read them before mailing them. Finally, if we are open to dialogue and interactions beyond the initial letter writing, we can model honoring multiple perspectives on an issue and maximize our students' opportunities to learn.

Indirect Service

Community service-learning—the integration of community service with the academic curriculum and structured reflection on the service experience—is another strategy for connecting students with opportunities to improve their community. Service learning for social justice does not adhere to a typical charity model, in which students just engage in service for those in need. Service-learning aimed at social change must also involve students in questioning the status quo, examining the root causes of injustice, and working *with*, rather than just *for*, those who experience injustice (Boyle-Baise, 2002; Kahne & Westheimer, 1996; Wade, 2000, 2001). "True service learning helps students make the connections between what they are studying in class and real-world issues. It engages students in action and reflection on important community, social, political, and environmental issues" (Berman, 1998, p. 31).

In-class service-learning projects often focus on indirect service experiences such as fund-raisers (e.g., bake sales, school stores, concession stands at sports events, plays, movies) and collection activities (e.g., books, money, canned goods, clothing, toys). These activities are relatively easy to coordinate, as students do not need to leave the school to complete them. Often school-based service-learning experiences grow out of problems in the school that students notice and decide to change. Upper elementary students might set up a schoolwide recycling program to eliminate the large volume of paper trash, create cross-age tutoring for struggling readers, or initiate a peer mediation program to address playground conflicts.

Other in-class service-learning activities focus on cross-cultural exchanges. For example, Rebecca's students adopted an orphanage in Tijuana, Mexico. "Because they do learn Spanish, they wrote a couple of letters to the students in the orphanage and then also sent them some bilingual books," explained Rebecca. Service-learning projects can also educate other students in the school about worthwhile social justice issues. For example, students studying the rain forest could put on a play to raise funds to donate to this cause.

While elementary schools across the nation typically include one or more indirect service activities as special events or enrichment activities, in the social justice classroom such experiences are central to the curriculum. We need to see projects that make a difference to others as "the main event, as jobs that replace, not just supplement, those tired old lesson plans" (Fried, 2001, p. 207).

School-Based Activism

Many opportunities to address meaningful problems and make significant change happen right within the school or on the playground. Students often find opportunities for social justice work in the daily life of school policies and practices as they encounter school rules or student behaviors they find unjust. For example, 9-year-old girls at one school successfully petitioned the principal to change a rule that allowed boys more playground space and better equipment. Teachers for social justice support students' initiatives to identify and work on solving social problems.

Activism has many positive benefits for students. It involves creative and critical thinking skills applied to real-life dilemmas that affect children's lives. Students feel empowered as they take on challenges and work together to solve complex problems. And there is no better way to engender student enthusiasm and commitment to learn than creating a situation in which they need facts or skills to solve a problem they care about.

Consider all of the skills the students in Molly's class developed as they worked on environmental issues in their school. Molly's first and second graders became concerned about the fact that Styrofoam trays were being discarded in the trash every day. "It was a waste," stated Molly. "We'd also been studying how you collect data and how you represent data in graphs, charts, and things like that, so they got some of their parents to help them and stand next to the trash barrels." After the students analyzed their findings they wrote a letter to request a meeting with the director of food services. Molly was very impressed with her students. They were confident and poised as they dialogued with the director and countered his arguments with creative proposals of their own. After he left, one little girl said, "the next time that students do a meeting like this you should have them think of more 'what if' questions before the person comes." While the students' advocacy did not bring about the desired result, Molly noted, "They didn't feel defeated at all. Even though they had done this very rigorous preparation, they recognized that they could have prepared even more. They had done all this very scientific and mathematical data gathering and used their literacy skills to get this stuff written down and assembled."

Molly's story effectively illustrates how planning for social action takes place day by day, rather than all at once at the beginning of a project, in part because students' discoveries, questions, and passions shape the course of the project. It's important that teachers do not completely plan or guide students' activism work in the direction that the teacher thinks is appropriate. Children need to muddle around in the issues they encounter in order to grow as critical thinkers and active learners (Pelo & Davidson, 2000).

While some might view this type of social justice work as taking valuable time away from the academic curriculum, Molly and many other teachers integrate academics—in this case, science and literacy—into students' social action experiences. At the same time, students learn valuable life skills in the process. Students learn how to identify a problem, to figure out who would support working on it, and what it would take to solve the problem. They then put their planning into action.

From conducting a schoolwide peace march in the wake of 9/11 to petitioning the district's superintendent about getting rid of standardized testing, to starting a teacher-student group focused on combating bullying, racism, and homophobia, elementary students can take on challenging and controversial issues in their schools. Our support for and dedication to student empowerment is critical, however. At best, this is a collaborative process in which we as teachers support and affirm students' interest, enthusiasm, and ideas while also providing guidance and asking questions that will lead students to a practical plan of action. Throughout the process, it is important to listen to students' ideas and concerns and to support their initiative and efforts as much as possible.

And when listening to students' voices, sometimes we may be surprised at who is most vocal or committed to taking action. The reluctant writer described in the beginning of this chapter became invested in his letter writing due to his interest in the cause he was promoting. Sue, an inner-city third-grade teacher, told how an unlikely pair of students took on the leadership in a social justice project. "One of them is a little girl who is the total classic well-behaved goody two-shoes," observed Sue, "and the other one was a kid who was like the class badass kind of boy." This unlikely duo paired up on their lunch break and collected signatures on a petition they submitted to the superintendent. This is a powerful civic lesson for students: that we can form alliances across our differences to work together toward a common goal.

Direct Service

Many service-learning projects give students the opportunity to extend their alliances with local community members. Frequently these projects center on direct service to people, animals, or the environment: Students can plant flowers, walk dogs at the animal shelter, read to senior citizens, or deliver and sort canned goods at the local food bank. Service-learning projects out in the community can be enriching experiences for students, teachers, and community members as everyone works together to improve the community.

While direct service activities require careful coordination on the part of teachers, student initiative and leadership are also essential. As teachers, we must attempt to balance support for students' interests and ideas with guidance toward completing a doable project.

Maximizing students' learning from their service experience entails going beyond integrating the project with academics. We must also foster students' abilities to reflect on and glean wisdom from their experience. It helps if we talk with children about the importance of reflective thinking and then give them some guiding questions to think about: What did I do? Why did I do it? What changes did it make in me? What change did it make in the world? Why do I think so? And where do I go from here? Talking or writing about questions such as these on a weekly basis helps to keep children focused and committed to the project and aids them in planning for the future.

Community Rallies and Marches

Another powerful strategy for social action in the community is attending a community rally or march. Students often enjoy making signs, participating in chants, and walking or riding their bikes along city streets with a group of people. However, there are several cautions relevant to students' participation in such events. First, we must be mindful of safety concerns; students should not be placed in a situation where they might be hurt by either those attending a rally or its onlookers. Second, most rallies and marches promote a certain point of view about a controversial or political issue. Students should have a choice as to whether or not they participate in such events and should never be coerced to take a particular point of view.

Despite these concerns, participation in a rally or march can be a meaningful way to connect students with one of our longstanding democratic practices: protest. Seren's students knew that he frequently attended community rallies to protest about various issues and they were pressuring him to take them along. When a rally for education funding at City Hall Park was announced, Seren sent a letter home and ended up with 13 students and a parent who planned to attend the evening event. The students stayed after school to make big colorful signs, and while the rally ended up being "kind of low energy," the students enjoyed waving their signs and chanting. When reporters and the president of the union came by, the students got a lot of positive attention. As the class returned to school to meet their parents, one student exclaimed, "Wow, that was our first rally but it won't be our last!" Upon arrival back at school, the students' parents were waiting. With elation, Seren described the meeting:

> So we came down the street chanting and waving signs, and while we were all the way down the block this whole group of parents that were there just burst out into applause and came running up and hugging their children. It was just such an incredibly powerful message to these kids of how important what they were doing was and how supported they were.

Seren concluded that this was "one of the most powerful experiences I've had with social justice teaching, particularly through the excitement it can generate and the opportunities for people to view themselves as activists." Pelo and Davidson (2000), early childhood antibias educators and authors, confirmed Seren's views: "Children do indeed want to be change-makers. As children go about their work of noticing differences, they also recognize the inequity inherent in some of those differences and want to do something about it. They want to be activists!" (p. 1).

While some of us might be hesitant to involve our students in a local rally or march due to the controversial nature of public demonstrations, our fears may be unfounded. As Bill Bigelow (2004), a longtime social justice teacher, observed, "the most powerful agent of censorship lives in our own heads, and we almost always have more freedom than we use" (pp. 125–126). Teaching for social justice engenders a passion for changing the world that can carry us beyond our fears and hesitations. And part of this passion is a commitment to giving our students the activist skills necessary to work for a socially just world as well. Bill and his colleagues are adamant about the importance of student activism in their teaching:

> If we ask children to critique the world but then fail to encourage them to act, our classrooms can degenerate into factories of cynicism. Part of a teacher's role is to suggest that ideas have real consequences and should be acted upon, and to offer students opportunities to do just that. (Editors of Rethinking Schools, 2003, p. 7)

Powerful experiences don't just happen on their own. An important aspect of social justice teaching is modeling being activists in our time outside of school and talking about these experiences with our students. This is not about indoctrinating students to adopt a certain perspective or to take up a specific issue. Rather, we are attempting to set an example of how one takes responsibility as a member of the community to try to make the world a better place for everyone. Supporting students' interests, seeking out suitable events for them to attend, and being willing to invite students to make their voices heard on controversial issues are all part of the recipe for powerful community experiences.

CONCLUSION

Connecting students to the world outside the classroom is an essential aspect of social justice education. In identifying issues of concern and practicing the skills of making a difference, students will begin to develop the commitment and ability to continue to address issues of injustice throughout their lives. And when community members enter the classroom to talk about their life experiences, students get a window into time periods and perspectives they might not have encountered otherwise. The mission of social studies education is to develop informed and active citizens and the practice of social justice work is one of the best means for reaching this goal.

Teaching Ideas

Guest Speaker

1. Look at your social studies curriculum for the upcoming school year. In which units could you incorporate a guest speaker? Who in the local community might be willing to talk to your students? In particular, think about speakers who could do one or more of the following: give students a personal understanding of an historic event or time period; present the perspective of someone from a group not featured in your social studies textbook; assist students with developing greater understanding and empathy for others; offer ideas for social action.

2. Invite the guest speaker to your classroom well in advance. Upper elementary students could be the ones to write and send the invitation. Be sure to let the guest speaker know how long you would like him or her to talk, how many and what age students will be present, and whether there will be time for questions.

3. Have students brainstorm questions or areas of interest for the guest speaker to address. Send these to your guest speaker well ahead of time to help the person prepare his or her remarks. With younger students, keep the guest speaker's time brief and encourage the speaker to include opportunities for dialogue as well as using photos, pictures, or other items to show.

4. A few days before the guest speaker is to arrive, give the person a call or an e-mail reminder to make sure everything is all set.

5. On the day the guest speaker is to arrive, ask one of the students to welcome the speaker and show him or her where to sit.

6. After the guest speaker leaves, talk with students about what they learned. Older students can write about their reflections, focusing on how what they learned helped to foster their understanding from a social justice perspective. Younger students can draw pictures and talk about the most interesting part of the speaker's talk. All ages of students should create and send thank-you notes to the speaker, perhaps including some of their written reflections or pictures.

Social Action in the School or Community

1. Social action opportunities arise when students look at their school and community through a social justice lens. Be alert to concerns of fairness or injustice mentioned by students. Use one or more of the following questions to foster this type of thinking: What do you think is unfair in our school or community? Does everyone have equal rights? If not, whose rights are being ignored or denied? Who is being left out? What problem, if solved, would lead to our community or school being a better place for everyone?

2. When students have identified an issue or problem that they care about, the next step is to gather more information about the issue. Ask students: Who do we need to talk to in order to learn about a variety of perspectives on this problem? Students could conduct a survey or interview their parents, other students in the school, or people in their neighborhood.

3. When students have a sufficient understanding of the problem, guide them in brainstorming ideas for what they could do to change the situation.

Before evaluating or deciding on a specific course of action, encourage students to come up with as many different ideas as they can.

4. Students next need to decide which idea(s) to put into action. Discuss which ideas are most feasible and desirable or have students evaluate each idea according to the following criteria: time, cost, interest, potential for impact.

5. With the action idea selected, have students develop a plan for making it happen. Older students should take leadership at this point, while younger students will need more teacher guidance and support to carry out their plan. Create a time line, a list of tasks and who will accomplish them, and a list of who else might be involved in assisting with the project.

6. Finally, after the project is completed, have students write and/or talk about their efforts. Was the project successful? If so, why? If not, why not? What did we learn from this experience that we could apply to future social action efforts?

8

Looking Forward

Social justice teaching makes a difference in the lives of students and communities by building inclusive and just classroom communities and engaging students in active learning on topics of importance. Social justice–oriented classrooms also give students opportunities for voice and choice in the classroom and facilitate their ability to engage in social action in the school and community. Elementary students in social justice classrooms develop empathy, self-esteem, and a firsthand knowledge of their abilities to work alongside others to address injustices as active and informed citizens.

Our qualities and actions as teachers for social justice lead not only to fulfilling our social justice goals, but also to being more effective teachers, especially for the nation's growing population of culturally and linguistically diverse students. Nieto (1999), citing many other scholars' findings (e.g., Ladson-Billings, 1994; Rose, 1995), noted that effective teachers of diverse students value students' identities, connect learning to students' lives, have high expectations of and commitment to their students, view parents and community members as partners in education, create a safe haven for learning, dare to challenge school and district bureaucracies, are resilient in the face of difficulties, use active learning strategies, are willing to experiment, view themselves as lifelong learners, and care about, respect, and love their students. These characteristics and behaviors are clearly evident in social justice teachers.

Unfortunately, the types of teachers Nieto describes and this book chronicles are not the norm in U.S. schools today. Yet if social justice teaching is to become more prevalent in our nation's schools, then systemic support is critical. If meaningful change is to happen, "it cannot remain at the level of individual teachers only. It needs to also happen at the level of entire schools and school districts" (Nieto, 1999, p. 47).

There are many strategies we can take to try to effect change on a larger scale. Invite a colleague to work with you on developing a social justice–oriented unit. Take or teach a social justice education workshop. Write about your social justice teaching for an educational publication. We can try to work "top-down" by changing public policy, speaking up at school board meetings, getting an advanced degree to work as an administrator, or working on writing the state standards. Or we can work with other teachers and parents, as Seren and Rob did, to create small schools that are aimed at social justice goals. Given our current standards-based educational environment, these efforts can be challenging and time consuming, and often met with resistance. Yet, as Kohl (1994a) asserted, "It is our job as educators to make schools work, and that requires taking up the struggle, within the system, to transform them" (p. 134).

Institutional change can be slow going. In the meantime, we must keep the flames for social justice burning in our hearts and those of our like-minded colleagues. Whether we work in a school committed to social justice or find ourselves without much support, there is work to be done. And if you feel like Laurie, that "finding an ally is really kind of like finding a pea under a mattress," take the risk to reach out to another teacher in your school. Finding one supportive colleague can make all the difference.

Melinda and Bruce are colleagues in a traditional public elementary school outside of Boston, Massachusetts. Both Melinda's and Bruce's life experiences have led them to strong personal convictions in the importance of teaching for social justice. Yet they also recognize the importance and power of collegial support. Melinda talked about the many ways she values Bruce as her ally:

> He watches and pays attention and he can identify times when I'm being targeted and he has all the tools he needs to confront them. The other ways that he's critical for me as an ally is that we sort of have committed to each other that when we want to call someone on their racism we don't have to feel that we have to call them on it instantly but we can go back to each other and talk it out. How would you handle this? What would you say? How does this sound? So that just gives you the courage and it gives you the sounding board and the practice to angle up to somebody. And these are typically people that you care

about who have racist assumptions that they haven't really considered. So you want to be even more careful with them. And for me, without that ally, that would be a lot harder.

Bruce's remarks indicated that he is equally appreciative of the support provided by Melinda:

If I'm frustrated about something administratively, I can just walk into her room and start talking and she knows what I'm talking about. We'd both be doing at least some of this if we didn't have each other, but it makes it a lot easier.

Clearly, the collegial support that Melinda and Bruce share developed over time. Yet it likely began in one moment, with one act, when one of them reached out to the other and took the risk to say what they believed about children and teaching and making a difference in the world. Taking the risk to ask for the other's support, or to suggest an initial collaboration in teaching led to a long-term and meaningful working relationship.

If you are the "Lone Ranger" for social justice in your school, take Rebecca's suggestion to post student work in the hallway, or follow Molly's advice to create a book discussion group that meets on evenings in teachers' homes. Or just walk down the hall, and invite another teacher to collaborate with you on a social justice–oriented unit or service-learning activity. Small steps to reach out to others may have surprising results, revealing that you are not alone in your concern for the world and your interest in doing something to help.

And if your attempts to find allies in your school are unsuccessful, take a social justice education course at a local university or join a national organization like Rethinking Schools. While social justice teachers in the United States are not the norm, there are teachers everywhere who believe in the possibility and potential of social change, within the schools, in the lives of children, and in our society. Reach out, find them, join them. And if your efforts seem insignificant in the face of the world's many injustices, keep in mind the following words of Dorothy Day (1963), human rights leader and founder of the Catholic Worker Movement:

Young people say, what is the sense of our small effort. They cannot see that we must lay one brick at a time, take one step at a time. . . . A pebble cast into a pond causes ripples that spread in all directions.

From our students to our community, to the world, the ripples of our teaching for social justice extend beyond time and space. We may not see the results of all our efforts, but we can be encouraged in the enthusiasm our students experience today as they speak up, question the status quo, come up with creative ideas, and work to create positive changes in their schools and communities. And we can trust that these experiences will give our students the skills, knowledge, and commitment they will need as adults to live empowered lives and build a socially just world.

Appendix A:
Social Justice Teaching Resources

(Compiled by Barbara Begin-Campbell and Paula O. Brandt, librarians in the University of Iowa Curriculum Laboratory.)

This list of resources includes children's books mentioned and used by social justice teachers interviewed as well as books added by Barbara Begin-Campbell and Paula Brandt (marked at end of citation with **). The children's books are organized in the following categories: picture storybooks, fiction, nonfiction picture books, and nonfiction books. We have also included sections on social justice–oriented professional books, curriculum guides, book awards, and Internet Web sites.

Picture Storybooks

Altman, L. J. (1993). *Amelia's road*. New York: Lee & Low.
　　The daughter of migrant farm workers creates a special place to represent home as she dreams of one day having a stable life.
Bang, M. (1999). *When Sophie gets angry—really, really angry*. New York: Blue Sky Press.
　　A very angry young girl handles a confrontation by leaving the scene, taking the time to regain her composure.
Birtha, B. (2005). *Grandmama's pride*. Morton Grove, IL: Albert Whitman.
　　When two African American girls from the North visit their grandmother in the South in 1956, they see how "separate but equal" operates, and see how their grandmother boycotts the public buses. **
Bunting, E. (1991). *Fly away home*. New York: Clarion.
　　A boy and his father live in an airport, where they try not to be noticed.
Cooney, B. (1982). *Miss Rumphius*. New York: Viking.
　　Toward the end of her life, an old woman plants lupines, which flourish, to make the world a more beautiful place.

Cronin, D. (2000). *Click, clack, moo: Cows that type.* New York: Simon & Schuster.
> *The cows and chickens go on strike when Farmer Brown won't give them electric blankets.*

Deedy, C. A. (2000). *The yellow star: Legend of King Christian X of Denmark.* Atlanta: Peachtree.
> *This story tells how King Christian X of Denmark defied the Nazis during World War II.* **

DiSalvo-Ryan, D. (2001). *A castle on Viola Street.* New York: HarperCollins.
> *A family gets their own house when they help renovate it along with others as part of a community program.* **

Hall, B. E. (2004). *Henry and the kite dragon.* New York: Philomel.
> *Chinese American and Italian American children living in New York in the 1920s narrowly avoid a confrontation when they discover they have been misunderstanding each other.* **

Heide, F. P. (1992). *Sam and the time of the troubles.* New York: Clarion.
> *This story describes the daily life of a 10-year-old Lebanese boy in Beirut who must live with his family in a basement shelter in the midst of bombings and violence.*

Hopkinson, D. (2003). *Girl wonder: A baseball story in nine innings.* New York: Atheneum.
> *This story tells how Alta Weiss became a baseball player on a semipro men's team in 1907.* **

Hopkinson, D. (1993). *Sweet Clara and the freedom quilt.* New York: Knopf.
> *A young girl uses scraps to stitch a quilt that can be used as map to guide slaves to freedom.*

Hopkinson, D. (2002). *Under the quilt of night.* New York: Atheneum.
> *A young girl describes the journey as she leads a group of slaves to freedom following clues and codes of the Underground Railroad.*

Johnson, D. B. (2003). *Henry climbs a mountain.* Boston: Houghton Mifflin.
> *Based on the life of Henry David Thoreau, Henry refuses to pay taxes that support slavery, and is sent to jail.* **

Katz, K. (1999). *The colors of us.* New York: Henry Holt.
> *As Lena and her mother walk through the neighborhood, they notice many beautiful shades of brown skin.*

Kurusa. (1995). *The streets are free.* New York: Annick Press.
> *A translation, this true story tells of the children of the barrio of San Jose de la Urbina, Venezuela, who have no place to play and join forces to confront the local government.*

Landowne, Y. (2004). *Sélavi, that is life: A Haitian story of hope.* El Paso, TX: Cinco Puntos Press.
> *A homeless boy on the streets of Haiti joins other street children, and*

together they build a home and a radio station where they can care for themselves and for other homeless children.**

Lionni, L. (1968). *Swimmy.* New York: Pantheon.
The little fishes learn they can outwit the big hungry fish when they work together as a team.

Lucas, E. (1997). *Cracking the wall: The struggles of the Little Rock Nine.* Minneapolis: Carolrhoda Books.
This book gives information on some of the activists during the Civil Rights Movement.

McDonough, Y. Z. (2002). *Peaceful protest: The life of Nelson Mandela.* New York: Walker.
This picturebook biography tells the story of South African leader Mandela, who worked tirelessly to end apartheid, even when a prisoner.**

McKissack, P. (2001). *Goin' someplace special.* New York: Atheneum.
A young African American girl must endure indignities and obstacles to get to one of the few integrated places in 1950s Nashville: the public library.

Mora, P. (1997). *Tomàs and the library lady.* New York: Knopf.
The young son of migrant laborers finds rest and discovers the world in books at a local public library.

Noguchi, R., & Jenks, D. (2001). *Flowers from Mariko.* New York: Lee & Low.
Living in a temporary trailer park after being released from the Japanese American internment camp, Mariko's family must find a way to recover hope and dignity.**

Parks, R., & Haskins, J. (1999). *I am Rosa Parks.* New York: Puffin.
Easy reader biography of Rosa Parks is told by Rosa to Jim Haskins.

Polacco, P. (2000). *The butterfly.* New York: Philomel.
During the Nazi occupation of France, Monique's mother hides a Jewish family in her basement and tries to help them escape to freedom.

Polacco, P. (1992). *Chicken Sunday.* New York: Philomel.
To thank Miss Eula for her wonderful Sunday chicken dinners, three children sell decorated eggs to buy her a beautiful Easter hat.

Polacco, P. (1992). *Mrs. Katz and Tush.* New York: Bantam.
A long-lasting friendship develops between a young African American boy and a lonely Jewish widow.

Polacco, P. (1988). *The keeping quilt.* New York: Simon & Schuster Books for Young Readers.
A homemade quilt ties together the lives of four generations of an immigrant Jewish family, remaining a symbol of their enduring love and faith.

Ringgold, F. (1993). *Dinner at Aunt Connie's house.* New York: Hyperion.
Melody meets not only her new adopted cousin but twelve inspiring African American women, who step out of their portraits and join the family for dinner.

Schroeder, A. (1996). *Minty: A story of young Harriet Tubman*. New York: Dial.
> *This fictionalized biography portrays the childhood attitudes and dreams of young Harriet leading to her own escape from slavery and tireless efforts helping others on the Underground Railroad.*

Seuss, Dr. (1961). *The Sneetches and other stories*. New York: Random House.
> *The unfortunate Sneetches are conned and taken advantage of due to their own pointless prejudice.*

Shea, P. D. (2003). *The carpet boy's gift*. Gardiner, ME: Tilbury House.
> *Based on the true story of Iqbal Masih, this is the story of a young Pakistani boy who is inspired to lead other children from bonded labor in a carpet factory to freedom and education.* **

Sisulu, E. (1996). *The day Gogo went to vote*. Boston: Little Brown.
> *Thembi accompanies her beloved great-grandmother as she leaves the house for the first time in years on the momentous day when black South Africans are allowed to vote for the first time.*

Skameta, A. (2000). *The composition*. Toronto: Groundwood.
> *Originally published in Venezuela, this story tells of how a boy, when told by government officials to write a composition about what his parents do in the evening, cleverly disguises the truth of their subversive activities.* **

Small, D. (1992). *Ruby Mae has something to say*. New York: Crown.
> *Tongue-tied Ruby Mae Foote fulfills her dream of speaking for world peace at the United Nations when her nephew invents a device to solve her speech problem.*

Tsuchiya, Y. (1988). *Faithful elephants*. Boston: Houghton Mifflin.
> *This story recounts how saddened keepers were forced to starve three elephants in a Tokyo zoo during World War II.*

Vander Zee, R. (2004). *Mississippi morning*. Grand Rapids, MI: Eerdmans.
> *Life changes forever when a boy discovers that his much admired father is a member of the KKK that has been terrorizing families in their community.* **

Waddell, M. (1991). *Farmer duck*. Cambridge, MA: Candlewick.
> *The farm animals unite to drive the lazy, abusive farmer away, then take over the farm operation themselves.*

Wahl, J. (2004). *Candy shop*. Watertown, MA: Charlesbridge.
> *A boy and his aunt comfort a new neighborhood shop owner from Taiwan when someone writes hateful words on the sidewalk.* **

Weatherford, C. B. (2005). *Freedom on the menu: The Greensboro sit-ins*. New York: Dial.
> *A young African American girl describes life in the segregated South and*

how her brother and his friends integrate the lunch counter in Greens-boro, North Carolina, in 1960.**

White, L. A. (2005). *I could do that: Esther Morris gets women the vote.* New York: Farrar, Straus, & Giroux.

This is the fictionalized biography of Esther Morris, the suffragist who worked to make Wyoming the first state to allow women to vote in 1869.**

Wiles, D. (2001). *Freedom summer.* New York: Atheneum.

In the South in 1964, a White boy and his African American friend are thrilled that the town swimming pool is now integrated; but when they see the pool has been filled with tar, they realize that prejudice still exists.**

Wyeth, S. D. (1998). *Something beautiful.* New York: Doubleday.

An African American girl searches her impoverished neighborhood for beauty, and finds it through its people.

Yang, B. (2004). *Hannah is my name.* Cambridge, MA: Candlewick.

A Chinese family emigrates to San Francisco and works illegally under threat of deportation while waiting for their green cards.**

Yin. (2001). *Coolies.* New York: Philomel.

A boy is told of his Chinese ancestors and how they put their lives in danger by coming to America in the mid-1860s to work on the transcontinental railroad.**

Yolen, J. (1992). *Encounter.* San Diego: Harcourt, Brace, Jovanovich.

In 1492, a Taino boy on what is now San Salvador recounts the arrival of Columbus and how that event destroyed the Taino way of life.

Yolen, J. (1992). *Letting Swift River go.* Boston: Little Brown.

The towns of the Swift River valley must be sacrificed to create a reservoir to supply growing Boston with water.

Fiction

Armstrong, W. H. (1969). *Sounder.* New York: Harper & Row.

Angry and humiliated when his sharecropper father is jailed for stealing food for the family, a young African American boy grows in courage and understanding by learning to read.

Byars, B. (1985). *Cracker Jackson.* New York: Viking Kestrel.

After attempting to save his ex-babysitter from wife abuse, Cracker Jackson gains an adult insight into the sadness of failed heroics.

Byars, B. (1977). *The pinballs.* New York: Harper & Row.

Three lonely foster children learn to care about themselves and each other.

Byars, B. (1970). *Summer of the swans*. New York: Viking.

A teenage girl gains new insight into herself and her family when her mentally retarded brother gets lost.

Clements, A. (2002). *The jacket*. New York: Simon & Schuster.

A short novel in which a White boy has to face his prejudices when he accuses an African American classmate of stealing a jacket. **

Creech, S. (2002). *Ruby holler*. New York: Joanna Cotler Books/Harper Collins.

Thirteen-year-old twins have grown up in a terrible orphanage, but their lives change forever when an eccentric older couple agrees to give them a home. **

Ellis, D. (2001). *The Breadwinner*. Toronto: Groundwood.

Living in Afghanistan where the Taliban rule, Parvana disguises herself as a boy so she can become the family breadwinner after her father is arrested. (Two sequels are Parvana's Journey *and* Mud City.*)* **

Garden, N. (2000). *Holly's secret*. Farrar, Straus, Giroux.

When she starts middle school, 12-year-old Holly decides to change her name and her image to hide the fact that her two moms are lesbians. **

Giff, P. R. (2002). *Pictures of Hollis Woods*. New York: Wendy Lamb Books.

A troublesome 12-year-old orphan, staying with an elderly artist who needs her, remembers the only other time she was happy in a foster home, with a family that truly seemed to care about her. **

Krensky, S. (1994). *The iron dragon never sleeps*. New York: Delacorte.

In 1867, 10-year-old Winnie meets a Chinese boy and discovers the role his people played in completing the transcontinental railroad.

Lowry, L. (1989). *Number the stars*. Boston: Houghton Mifflin.

Ten-year-old Annemarie courageously aids the Resistance and helps shelter her Jewish friend from the Nazis during the German occupation of Denmark.

Moss, M. P. (2000). *Hannah's journal: The story of an immigrant girl*. San Francisco: Silver Whistle/Harcourt.

A 10-year-old Jewish girl recounts the story of her journey to America in her journal as she flees the pogroms and violence in the Russian shtetl where she and her family live.

Naidoo, B. (1985). *Journey to Jo'burg: A South African story*. New York: Lippincott.

Two African children walk and hitch their way to Johannesburg to find their mother, learning about the horrors of apartheid on their journey.

Napoli, D. J. (2005). *The king of Mulberry Street*. New York: Wendy Lamb Books.

In 1892, a 9-year old stowaway from Italy arrives in New York and must learn to survive the perils of street life while avoiding the padrones, *men who pay passage for homeless children then force them to work off debts.* **

Park, L. S. (2005). *Project mulberry*. New York: Clarion.
A Korean American girl and her friend Patrick ask an African American man for leaves from his mulberry tree for their silk-worm project as they learn not just about silkworms, but also about tolerance, prejudice, friendship, patience, and more. **

Paterson, K. (1996). *Jip: His story*. New York: Lodestar.
While living on a Vermont poor farm during 1855 and 1856, Jip learns of his interracial identity as son of a runaway slave. **

Pearsall, S. (2005). *Crooked river*. New York: Knopf.
Living in 1812 frontier Ohio, a young girl is afraid that an innocent Chippewa man being held for the murder of a White trapper is going to be executed **

Rodman, M. A. (2004). *Yankee girl*. New York: Farrar, Straus, & Giroux.
When Alice moves with her FBI father to Mississippi in 1964, she is torn between trying to get "in" with the popular girls and befriending Valerie, an African American girl, one of two students integrating the school. **

Steig, W. (1973). *The real thief*. New York: Farrar, Straus, & Giroux.
Gawain the goose is deserted by his friends after being unjustly convicted of stealing from his beloved king, but the real thief heeds his conscience and corrects the injustice.

Taylor, M. D. (1976). *Roll of thunder, hear my cry*. New York: Dial.
An African American family living in the South during the Great Depression struggles to retain their humanity and dignity in the face of prejudice and discrimination.

Taylor, M. D. (1987). *The gold Cadillac*. New York: Dial.
Two African American girls living in the North are proud of their family's beautiful new Cadillac until they take it on a visit to the South and encounter racial prejudice for the first time.

Taylor, M. D. (1975). *Song of the trees*. New York: Dial.
During the Depression, powerful lumbermen attempt to take advantage of the Logans' poverty by cutting down their centuries-old forest.

Wilson, N. H. (2001). *Mountain pose*. New York: Farrar Straus, & Giroux.
When her estranged grandmother dies, a 12-year-old girl inherits an old Vermont farm and a set of diaries which reveal a cycle of abuse, but provide Ellie with inspiration for understanding and forgiveness. **

Nonfiction Picture Books

Brown, D. (2004). *Kid blink beats the world*. Brookfield, CT: Roaring Brook.
Children who were street newspaper deliverers successfully went on strike against the unfair labor practices of the New York newspaper publishers in 1899. **

Cherry, L. (1992). *A river ran wild: An environmental history.* San Diego: Harcourt, Brace, & Jovanovich.

> *The Nashua River went from being a clear river to a polluted one until rescued by local Massachusetts activists.*

Coles, R. (1995). *The story of Ruby Bridges.* New York: Scholastic.

> *Six-year-old Ruby Bridges must face the hostility of parents of White children as she becomes the first African American girl to integrate an elementary school in New Orleans in 1960.*

Demi. (2001). *Gandhi.* New York: Margaret McElderry.

> *This is a picturebook biography of the peace-loving leader from India who inspired Martin Luther King, Jr., Nelson Mandela, and many others.* **

Ellis, D. (2005). *Our stories, our songs: African children talk about AIDS.* Markham, ON: Fitzhenry & Whiteside.

> *Facts about the AIDS pandemic in Africa are interspersed with the stories of individual children in Malawi and Zambia as they tell how AIDS has affected their lives.* **

Fox, M. (1997). *Whoever you are.* San Diego: Harcourt Brace.

> *Despite the differences between people around the world, there are similarities that join us together, such as pain, joy, and love.*

Hennessy, B. G. (2005). *Because of you: A book of kindness.* Cambridge, MA: Candlewick Press.

> *Every single person helps make the world a kinder and more peaceful place.* **

Houston, G. (1992). *My great aunt Arizona.* New York: HarperCollins.

> *An Appalachian girl grows up to become a teacher who influences generations of schoolchildren.*

Kindersley, B., & Kindersley, A. (1997). *Children just like me.* London: Dorling Kindersley.

> *Photographs document the lives of children and their families in 30 countries.*

Krull, K. (2003). *Harvesting hope.* San Diego: Harcourt.

> *This is the biography of Cesar Chavez, who worked to improve the conditions of migrant workers.* **

McDonough, Y. Z. (2002). *Peaceful protest: The life of Nelson Mandela.* New York: Walker.

> *This picturebook biography tells the story of South African leader Mandela, who worked tirelessly to end apartheid, even when a prisoner.* **

Rappaport, D. (2001). *Martin's big words: The life of Martin Luther King, Jr.* New York: Hyperion.

> *The life of Dr. King is revealed through his speeches.* **

Raven, M. T. (2005). *Let them play.* Chelsea, MI: Sleeping Bear.

In 1955 the one and only black Little League program in South Carolina faces prejudice and discrimination at the local, state, and national level. **

Ringgold, F. (1999). *If a bus could talk: The story of Rosa Parks.* New York: Simon & Schuster.

This is the biography of Rosa Parks, an African American civil rights worker whose refusal to give up her seat on a bus led to the 1955 Montgomery Bus Boycott in Alabama.

Scholes, K. (1990). *Peace begins with you.* San Francisco: Little Brown.

This book shows why peace is important in our lives, explaining why conflicts occur and how they can be resolved in positive ways.

Smith, D. J. (2002). *If the world were a village: A book about the world's people.* Toronto: Kids Can Press.

This book reduces the world's population to 100 people, then tells how many of those people are members of certain religions, are literate, are starving, and so on. **

Spier, P. (1980). *People.* Garden City, NY: Doubleday.

This book celebrates the differences in people and culture around the world.

Zak, M. (1992). *Save my rainforest.* Volcano, CA: Volcano Press.

Eight-year-old Omar Castillo fulfills his dream of visiting the endangered rain forest of southern Mexico and wins an audience with the president of Mexico to express his concern.

Nonfiction Books

Bausum, A. (2004). *With courage and cloth: Winning the fight for a woman's right to vote.* Washington, DC: National Geographic.

The long battle fought by women to get the right to vote is discussed, with special emphasis on activist Alice Paul. **

Coerr, E. (1977). *Sadako and the 1,000 paper cranes.* New York: Putnam.

A child in Hiroshima with radiation-induced leukemia attempts to fold one thousand paper cranes believing in a legend that says a sick person will become healthy if he does so.

Cooper, M. L. (2002). *Remembering Manzanar: Life in a Japanese relocation camp.* New York: Clarion.

What life was like in a relocation camp is described by using information from diaries, school newspapers, journals, and other primary sources. **

Crowe, C. (2003). *Getting away with murder: The true story of the Emmett Till case.* New York: Phyllis Fogelman.

A 14-year-old African American boy was murdered in Mississippi in 1955, and his white murderers were acquitted.**

Frank, O., & Pressler, M. (Eds.). (1995). *Diary of a young girl: Anne Frank.* New York: Doubleday.

> *The day-to-day life of a Jewish girl is presented in her diary while she hid in an attic in Nazi-occupied Holland for 2 years.*

Fritz, J. (1976). *What's the big idea, Ben Franklin?* New York: Coward, McCann, & Geoghegan.

> *This is a brief biography of the eighteenth-century printer, inventor, and statesman who played an influential role in the early history of the United States.*

Hoose, P. M. (2001). *We were there, too!: Young people in U.S. history.* New York: Farrar, Straus, & Giroux.

> *This book presents biographies of dozens of children and teens who played important roles in American history, including child laborers and civil rights workers.***

Hopkinson, D. (2003). *Shutting out the sky: Life in the tenements of New York, 1880–1915.* New York: Orchard.

> *The lives of five immigrants living in miserable conditions in New York's Lower East Side is documented.***

Lester, J. (1998). *From slave ship to freedom road.* New York: Dial Books.

> *Twenty paintings by Rod Brown portray the hardships of African American slaves, with meditations about endurance, fear, hope, and freedom.*

Curriculum Guides

Bigelow, B., Christensen, L., Karp, S., Miner, B., & Peterson, B. (Eds.). (1994, 2001). *Rethinking our classrooms: Teaching for equity and justice* (Vols. 1–2). Milwaukee, WI: Rethinking Schools.

> *Articles, curriculum ideas, lesson plans, poetry, and resources are designed to help teachers promote the values of community, justice, and equality in their classrooms.*

Thoman, E., & Wright, M. (Eds.). (1995). *Beyond blame challenging violence in the media: A media literacy program for community education.* Los Angeles, CA: Center for Media Literacy.

> *This elementary unit consists of a video program and printed materials designed to explore alternatives to violent entertainment.*

Derman-Sparks, L., & the Anti-Bias Curriculum Task Force. (1989). *Anti-bias curriculum: Tools for empowering young children.* Washington, DC: National Association for the Education of Young People.

> *This book describes the philosophy, suggestions for adaptation, and activities for creating a nonbiased curriculum.*

Lee, E., Menkart, D., & Okazawa-Rey, M. (Eds.). (1998). *Beyond heroes and holidays: A practical guide to K–12 anti-racist, multicultural education and staff development.* Washington, DC: Network of Educators for the Americas.

> *This interdisciplinary guide for teachers, administrators, students, and parents offers lessons and readings about how to make a curriculum nonracist and nonbiased.*

Lewis, B. A. (1991). *The kid's guide to social action: How to solve the social problems you choose—and turn creative thinking into positive action.* Minneapolis, MN: Free Spirit.

> *This resource guide is designed for children to learn political action skills that can help them make a difference in solving social problems at the community, state, and national levels.*

Schniedewind, N., & Davidson, E. (1983). *Open minds to equality: A sourcebook of learning activities to promote race, sex, class, and age equity.* Englewood Cliffs, NJ: Prentice-Hall.

> *These activities for elementary and middle school teachers help students recognize and change inequities based on sex, race, age, and competitive individualism.*

Children's Book Awards

The Once Upon A World Children's Book Award: Simon Wiesenthal Center & Museum of Tolerance (http://www.wiesenthal.com/site/pp.asp?c=fwLYKnN8LzH&b=242746)

Jane Adams Award: Jane Adams Peace Association and Women's International League for Peace and Freedom (http://www.janeaddamspeace.org/index.asp)

Carter G. Woodson Book Awards: National Council for the Social Studies (http://www.socialstudies.org/awards/woodson/)

The Pura Belpré Award: American Library Association (http://www.ala.org/Template.cfm?Section=bookmediaawards&template=/ContentManagement/ContentDisplay.cfm&ContentID=102627)

Coretta Scott King Award: American Library Association (http://www.ala.org/ala/emiert/corettascottkingbookawards/corettascott.htm)

Internet Web Sites

Educators for Social Responsibility (http://www.esrnational.org/home.htm)
Open Circle (http://www.open-circle.org)
Radical Teacher (http://www.radicalteacher.org/)
Rethinking Schools (http://rethinkingschools.org)
Southern Poverty Law Center's Teaching Tolerance Program (http://www
    .teachingtolerance.org)
Teaching for Change (http://www.teachingforchange.org/)

Appendix B:
Description of the Research

I conducted this research study between the summer of 2001 and the fall of 2004. The 40 teacher participants in this study range in age from 24 to 63, with a mean age of 43.8 years. Years of teaching range from 2 to 35 years, with a mean of 13.3 years taught. Almost half of the teachers ($n = 18$) have taught 10 years or less; nine of the teachers have been teaching for more than twenty years. Most teachers have had a broad range of experience within the elementary grades, and several have taught preschool, middle, or high school as well. Looking at the most recent elementary grade level taught at the time of the study for each teacher, 20 taught at the primary (K–3) level, 16 at the intermediate (4–6) level, and four identified their teaching positions as K–6.

The teacher participants represent a more diverse sample than one would find in the population of elementary teachers in the United States as a whole. There are 34 women and 6 men; almost a quarter identified their ethnicity as other than white ($n = 9$, 2 Puerto Rican, 2 Mexican American, 4 African American, and 1 Arab American). Several teachers identified themselves as being from targeted or oppressed groups in society (gay, lesbian, Jewish, poor). Twenty-three of the teachers taught in urban settings, 13 in suburban towns, and 4 in rural communities. Following is a list of the participants' teaching locations. The sites are listed alphabetically, one teacher at each site, unless I have indicated otherwise.

Boston, MA	Lafayette, CO	Northampton, MA
Boulder, CO	Los Angeles, CA	Oakland, CA
Canandaigua, NY	Madison, WI	Philadelphia, PA (2)
Champaign, IL	Milwaukee, WI	San Francisco, CA
Chicago, IL (4)	New York City—	Seattle, WA
Cedar Falls, IA	the Bronx (3)	Southampton, MA
Concord, MA (2)	New York City—	Tampa, FL (2)
Crossville, AL	Harlem (2)	Toledo, OH
Galleton, TN	North Adams,	Urbana, IL
Hartford, CT (2)	MA (3)	Washington, DC
Jamaica Plain, MA		

Teachers self-selected for this study by responding to an e-mail invitation. E-mail messages were sent to the following organizations and individuals to enlist their assistance in finding elementary school teachers who teach for and/or about social justice who would be interested in participating in the study. The individuals listed are teacher educators (and a few teachers) who have published on teaching for social justice.

The organizations included: College and University Faculty Assembly of the National Council for the Social Studies (CUFA), Social Justice Special Interest Group; Educators for Social Responsibility (ESR); Facing History Ourselves, Institute for Democracy in Education (IDE); National Association for Multicultural Education (NAME); National Coalition of Educational Activists (NCEA); National Council for the Social Studies (NCSS); National Society for Experiential Education (NSEE), Social Justice Special Interest Group; National Youth Leadership Council (NYLC); Network of Educators on the Americas (NECA); and Rethinking Schools. Individuals included: Maurianne Adams, William Ayers, Sam Crowell, Dave Donahue, Colin Green, Edith Guyton, Deborah Habib, Jane Hammat Kowalski, Todd Jennings, Margot Kennard, Andra Makler, Sonia Nieto, Susan Noffke, Masha Rudman, Mara Sapon-Shevin, and Tracey Seabolt.

Two factors in the recruitment process assisted with locating teachers who do, in fact, teach for and/or about social justice. First, each teacher participant was connected with either a social justice education organization or a teacher educator who had published on social justice education. Second, a brief description of social justice education was included in the e-mail invitation so that teachers had some idea of the study's focus. The following is the text of the e-mail message sent to prospective participants.

> I am currently seeking elementary school teachers who teach for social justice who might like to participate in a focus group interview with several other elementary school teachers at or near the school where they teach. Participants would need to sign a consent form to participate in this research study, and they would also receive $25 for the one-hour interview.
>
> Social justice education empowers students to analyze the root causes of injustice, promote equal opportunity for all people, and learn from multiple perspectives on an issue or topic within a collaborative, experiential approach to teaching and learning. I am particularly interested in working with teachers who teach for social justice through their elementary social studies curriculum.
>
> Please contact me with your name and e-mail address (or the names and e-mail addresses or individual teachers who you think might be interested in this opportunity), and I will send you additional information. If you or teachers you know have additional questions about this project, they can contact me by phone or by e-mail.
>
> I am excited about learning more about teaching for social justice and connecting teachers who are involved in this effort with each other. This collaboration will hopefully lead to publications that will provide new directions for the field of elementary social studies.
>
> Sincerely,
> Rahima Wade
> Associate Professor of Elementary
>   Social Studies
> The University of Iowa

Each teacher participated in a one-to-two-hour interview, either individually or in a small focus group. Following a semi-structured format, I used a set of specific questions to frame the interviews (Rubin & Rubin, 1995). These are the teacher interview questions:

1. Describe your teaching situation, grade level, subjects taught, type of school and community, and so forth.
2. Describe a unit or lesson where you were teaching for social justice.
3. What does "social justice" mean to you?
4. What does "teaching for social justice" mean to you?
5. Are there particular strategies that you feel are essential in teaching for social justice?
6. Are there particular topics or subjects that you feel are essential in teaching for social justice?
7. Why do you teach for social justice? What is your motivation?
8. What are your goals in teaching for social justice?
9. What are the benefits for you and/or your students in teaching for social justice?
10. Who or what supports you in teaching for social justice?
11. What are the challenges or difficulties for you and/or your students in teaching for social justice?
12. Who or what makes your teaching for social justice difficult?
13. What materials, curricula, or other resources do you find especially useful?
14. What types of resources do you wish you had?
15. Is there anything else you would like to share about teaching for social justice?

Each teacher also completed an information sheet that included their name, age, gender, ethnicity, number of years teaching, past teaching positions, present teaching position, and relevant life experiences and interests in regard to teaching for social justice.

When possible, I interviewed teachers in person at their school sites; this was the case for 13 of the teachers. I interviewed 5 other teachers face-to-face in their homes or at professional conferences. Due to limitations on time and funding to travel, I conducted the remainder of the interviews over the phone. I tape-recorded all interviews and I, along with a graduate student and professional staff in the University of Iowa College of Education, transcribed the tapes verbatim.

A grant from the Fund for the Advancement of Social Studies Education (FASSE) and the College and University Faculty Assembly (CUFA) of the National Council for the Social Studies enabled me to observe in two teachers' classrooms for 15 hours each. These teachers were located in Northampton, Massachusetts, and Cedar Falls, Iowa. The grant also funded 15 hours of focus group meetings during one weekend in October 2004 in Iowa City, Iowa. In addition to the two teachers I observed, teachers from the Bronx, NY; Boston, MA; Denver, CO; Philadelphia, PA; Toledo, OH; Urbana, IL; Madison, WI; and Seattle, WA attended. The teachers were selected based on the quality of their initial interviews as well as geographic, ethnic, and grade-level diversity. Qualitative data analysis focused on understanding the various factors that influence teachers' experiences of teaching for and about social justice. If you have questions about this study beyond the information provided here, please e-mail me at rahima-wade@uiowa.edu.

References

Adams, M., Bell, L. A., & Griffin, P. (Eds.). (1997). *Teaching for diversity and social justice: A sourcebook*. New York: Routledge.

Akenson, J. E. (1987). Historical factors in the development of elementary social studies: Focus on the expanding environments. *Theory and Research in Social Education, 15*(3), 155–171.

Ayers, W. (2004). *Teaching the personal and political: Essays on hope and justice*. New York: Teachers College Press.

Berger, P. (1977). Are human rights universal? *Commentary* (New York), *64*(3), 60–63.

Berman, S. (1998). The bridge to civility: Empathy, ethics, and service. *The School Administrator, 55*(5), 27–32.

Bigelow, B. (2004). The desecration of Studs Terkel: Fighting censorship and self-censorship. In K. D. Salas, R. Tenorio, S. Walters, & D. Weiss (Eds.), *The new teacher book: Finding purpose, balance, and hope during your first years in the classroom* (pp. 123–126). Milwaukee, WI: Rethinking Schools.

Bigelow, B., Christensen, L., Karp, S., Miner, B., & Peterson, B. (Eds.). (1994). *Rethinking our classrooms: Teaching for equity and justice*. Milwaukee, WI: Rethinking Schools.

Boyle-Baise, M. (2002). *Multicultural service learning: Educating teachers in diverse communities*. New York: Teachers College Press.

Burke-Hengen, M., & Smith, G. (2000). Students in the soup kitchen. In A. Makler & R. S. Hubbard (Eds.), *Teaching for justice in the social studies classroom: Millions of intricate moves* (pp. 99–115). Portsmouth, NH: Heinemann.

Christensen, L., & Karp, S. (Eds.). (2003). *Rethinking school reform: Views from the classroom*. Milwaukee, WI: Rethinking Schools.

Cochran-Smith, M. (2004). *Walking the road: Race, diversity, and social justice in teacher education*. New York: Teachers College Press.

Day, D. (1963). *Loaves and Fishes*. New York: Harper & Row.

Editors of Rethinking Schools. (2003). Rethinking our classrooms: Teaching for equity and justice. In L. Christensen & S. Karp (Eds.), *Rethinking school reform: Views from the classroom* (pp. 3–9). Milwaukee, WI: Rethinking Schools.

Fleischman, P. (1988). *Joyful noise: Poems for two voices.* New York: HarperCollins.

Fried, R. L. (2001). *The passionate teacher.* Boston: Beacon Press.

Furman, G. C., & Gruenewald, D. A. (2004). Exploring the landscape of social justice: A critical ecological analysis. *Educational Administration Quarterly, 40*(1), 47–76.

Grant, S. G. (1997). Opportunities lost: Teachers learning about the New York state social studies framework. *Theory and Research in Education, 25*(3), 259–287.

Gratz, D. B. (2000). High standards for whom? *Phi Delta Kappan, 81,* 681–687.

Haynes, C., Chaltain, S., Ferguson, J. E., Hudson, D., & Thomas, O. (2003). *The First Amendment in Schools.* Alexandria, VA: Association for Supervision and Curriculum Development.

Houser, N. O. (1995). Social studies on the back burner: Views from the field. *Theory and Research in Social Education, 23*(2), 147–168.

Kahne, J., &Westheimer, J. (1996). In the service of what? The politics of service learning. *Phi Delta Kappan, 77*(9), 593–599.

Kohl, H. (1994a). *"I won't learn from you" and other thoughts on creative maladjustment.* New York: The New Press.

Kohl, H. (1994b). The politics of children's literature: What's wrong with the Rosa Parks myth? In B. Bigelow, L. Christensen, S. Karp, B. Miner, & B. Peterson (Eds.), *Rethinking our classrooms: Teaching for equity and justice.* (pp. 137–140). Milwaukee, WI: Rethinking Schools.

Kumashiro, K. K. (2004). *Against common sense: Teaching and learning toward social justice.* New York: Routledge-Farmer.

Ladson-Billings, G. (1992). But that's just good teaching! The case for culturally relevant pedagogy. *Theory Into Practice, 34*(3), 159–165.

Ladson-Billings, G. (1994). *The dreamkeepers: Successful teachers of African American children.* San Francisco: Jossey-Bass.

Levine, D. (1995). Building a vision of educational reform. In D. Levine, R. Lowe, B. Peterson, & R. Tenario (Eds.), *Rethinking schools: An agenda for change.* New York: The New Press.

Levstik, L., & Barton, K. (2005). *Doing history: Investigating with children in elementary and middle schools.* Mahwah, NJ: Lawrence Erlbaum.

Marx, K. (1972). Critique of the Gotha Program. In R. C. Tucker (Ed.), *The Marx-Engles Reader* (pp. 525–541). New York: Norton. (Original work published 1875)

Nieto, S. (1999). *The light in their eyes: Creating multicultural learning communities*. New York: Teachers College Press.

Nieto, S. (2003). *What keeps teachers going?* New York: Teachers College Press.

Pelo, A., & Davidson, F. (2000). *That's not fair! A teacher's guide to activism with young children*. St. Paul, MN: Redleaf Press.

Pipkin, C. W. (1927). *The idea of social justice*. New York: MacMillan.

Rose, M. (1995). *Possible lives: The promise of public education in America*. New York: Penguin Books.

Rubin, H. J., & Rubin, I. S. (1995). *Qualitative interviewing: The art of hearing data*. Thousand Oaks, CA: Sage.

Villegas, A. M., & Lucas, T. (2002). *Educating culturally responsive teachers*. Albany: State University of New York Press.

Vygotsky, L. S. (1978). *Mind in society: The development of higher psychological processes* (M. Cole et al., Trans.). Cambridge, MA: Harvard University Press. (Original works published 1935–1966)

Wade, R. (2000). Beyond charity: Service learning for social justice. *Social Studies and the Young Learner, 12*(4), 6–9.

Wade, R. C. (2001). ". . . And justice for all": Community service-learning for social justice [Issue paper]. Denver, CO: Education Commission of the States.

Wade, R. C. (2004). Citizenship for social justice. *Kappa Delta Pi Record, 40*(2), 64–68.

Willoughby, W. W. (1900). *Social Justice*. New York: MacMillan.

Young, I. M. (1990). *Justice and the politics of difference*. Princeton, NJ: Princeton University Press.

Index